COMET!

The Story Behind Halley's Comet

by

Greg Walz-Chojnacki

AstroMedia/Gareth Stevens

1985

To My Father
Who just missed Halley the last time around.

Book design and production by Pat LaBrecque

Cover painting by Mark Paternostro

The star maps in this book were created using Mapmaker
software copyright © 1984 Richard Berry

First published in 1985 by

AstroMedia Corp.
625 E. St. Paul Ave., Milwaukee, WI 53202
and

Gareth Stevens, Inc.
7221 W. Green Tree Rd., Milwaukee, WI 53223

Copyright © 1985 AstroMedia Corp.

Library of Congress Cataloging in Publication Data
Walz-Chojnacki, Greg, 1954 -
    Comet!: the story behind Halley's comet.
    Summary: Explains the nature of comets, what is known
about Halley's comet, and various countries' plans to study it
in 1985 and 1986. Makes suggestions for maximum viewing
enjoyment.
    Includes index.
    1. Halley's comet — Juvenile literature. [1. Halley's comet.
2. Comets] I. Title
QB723.H2W35 1985   523.6′4   85-15632
ISBN 0-913135-03-8
ISBN 0-918831-51-2 (lib. bdg.)

Contents

Introduction

There are two reasons it's fun to look into the night sk[...] the patterns of light and motion we find beyond our planet are among the most beautiful nature has to offer. Second, when we ask what those patterns of light *really are*, we discover some of the strangest and most fascinating things our minds can encounter.

A comet provides the perfect opportunity to enjoy the double fun of astronomy. Nothing matches the sight of a comet's glowing head and wispy tail hanging above the horizon. And because comets are so unusual, it's natural to wonder *why* they're so different. Why do they appear so suddenly — then disappear just as quickly? What are they really? Where do they come from?

In the following pages, you'll see that the mystery of comets matches their beauty. In fact, comets are among the most challenging puzzles of astronomy. As you find out what we know — and don't know — about comets, you'll see why astronomers are so excited about Comet Halley.

Of course, *you're* excited about the chance to see a comet! One aim of this book is to help you get the best possible look at Halley's Comet.

You may have heard that the coming appearance of Comet Halley is going to be disappointing. Nothing could be further from the truth. This may be the best return of Halley ever: With our ability to reach into space, we have the opportunity to make many new discoveries about comets. A second purpose of this book is to help you share the excitement of these discoveries.

As you observe Halley, you may discover a third — perhaps the most important — reason people enjoy stargazing. Looking into the vast universe, you may suddenly find yourself thinking about our own planet from a completely new and satisfying point of view. If you have this experience while observing Comet Halley, you'll find that this once-in-a-lifetime return is just the beginning of a lifetime of discovering the universe and our place in it.

While only the author's name appears on the cover of this book, most of the staff of AstroMedia Corp. contributed to this project; my thanks especially to Nancy Mack, Pat LaBrecque, Jane Borth Lucius, Mary Algozin, Susan Poole, and Mary MacAdam for their help (and patience!). Thanks also to my friend Frank Reddy for both his excellent maps and excellent advice. Dan Green of the Harvard Astrophysical Center contributed helpful comments on early drafts of the manuscript. Finally, special credit goes to Ruth Freitag of the Library of Congress, whose compilation of historical images proved so useful.

Chapter 1

An Ancient Puzzle

A painting of Montezuma, King of the Aztecs, watching the comet that "foretold" his defeat by the Spanish conquistador Cortez.

From *Los Tlacuilos de Frey Diego Duran*, copyright © 1975 Carton y Papel de Mexico

Imagine that you are living 3,000 years ago. You know the sky well, and watch it for important signs, such as the coming and going of the seasons. Besides the star groups you tell stories about, you are familiar with the four or five "wandering stars." The night sky is a friendly place, and with all the unpredictability of your daily life, it's nice to know you can at least count on the orderly motions and patterns of the heavens.

But tonight you look up to see something new in the sky. The sight bothers you, for this odd visitor has no place in the familiar patterns, and its weird fuzziness and faint, swordlike tail are like nothing you've ever seen before.

You rush to the temple to hear what the priests have to say. They seem as nervous and uncertain as you feel, but their predictions of bad fortune make sense to you. After all, just as the horsemen of the north bring chaos to your land, this queer invader of the night may destroy the one dependable thing in

This picture from a 17th century book on comets shows three ideas about comets: that they lie below the Moon (left); that they orbit the Sun in curved paths (center); and that they travel in straight lines (right).

your life, the order of the heavens. And who knows how those changes might affect the Earth?

* * *

It is not hard to understand why comets were so frightening and puzzling to our ancestors. Nothing in the sky looks quite like a comet, and a comet's movement through the heavens is unlike that of stars or planets. Superstitious people would naturally find comets troubling.

For centuries, comets were seen as signs of coming disaster. Halley's Comet alone managed to get blamed for some impressive mishaps: the fall of Jerusalem in 70 A.D.; a plague that occurred in 141; the defeat of Attila the Hun in 451 (which wasn't bad for everyone!); the defeat in 1066 of Harold II of England by William of Normandy (now known as William the Conqueror — and probably a *fan* of comets); and the invasion of Europe by the Turks in 1456.

This 19th century French cartoon captures the terror that comets held for our ancestors.

The sudden, unpredictable appearance of comets made it difficult for ancient observers to study them scientifically. But not all ancient ideas about comets were totally ridiculous. Some Babylonians suspected that comets were orbiting celestial bodies like planets. Greek philosophers, whom many consider the first scientists, also had some reasonable ideas about comets. Many felt that they were celestial objects, occupying the heavens with the planets. Some believed comets were planets, others thought of them as groups of stars. The ancient Greeks, who contributed so much to western civilization, gave us the word comet, from their term *kometes aster*, ''hairy star.''

The Ancient ''Authority''

Unfortunately, the Greek philosopher who had the greatest influence on science had a lot of mistaken ideas about astronomy. This philosopher, Aristotle (AIR-iss-ta-tull), believed that the Earth lay at the center of the Solar System, and that all heavenly objects were divine. The orbits of planets, Aristotle reasoned, had to be circles, since only this ''perfect'' shape was suitable for the heavens.

The unpredictable comet had no place in the divine order of the heavens seen by Aristotle. Instead, he believed that comets were part of Earth's weather, caused by ''fiery exhalations'' of the atmosphere. Aristotle believed these exhalations caused droughts and high winds, so comets were ''scientifically'' proven to be signs of these natural disasters.

Aristotle's astronomical ideas were not challenged for nearly 2,000 years. The proof that comets were not in the atmosphere finally came when the Danish astronomer Tycho Brahe (TIE-koe BRAH-hay) carefully measured the position of a comet in 1577, and showed that it lay far beyond the Moon.

Tycho's brilliant assistant, Johannes Kepler, helped overthrow Aristotle's ideas about the Solar System. Kepler's great discovery was that planetary orbits are not perfect circles, but ellipses (see ''Let's Make an Ellipse''). But while Kepler successfully described

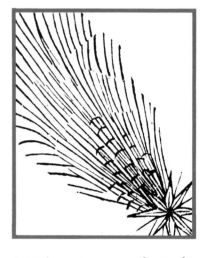

A 15th century woodcut of the appearance of Halley's Comet in 684 A.D.

Not everybody felt that comets were horrible omens. In his painting, "The Adoration of the Magi," the 14th century artist Giotto di Bondone used Halley's Comet to represent the Star of Bethlehem.

Courtesy European Space Agency

Edmond Halley, who first predicted the return of the comet that bears his name.

The Royal Society

Even as late as 1909, when this picture appeared in *Pearson's Magazine*, people worried that a comet could cause disaster from millions of miles away.

Courtesy Library of Congress

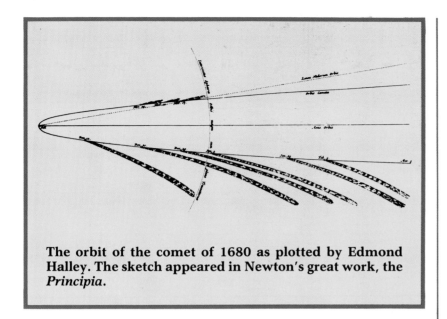

The orbit of the comet of 1680 as plotted by Edmond Halley. The sketch appeared in Newton's great work, the *Principia*.

Let's Make an Ellipse

the positions and motions of the planets, he did not understand the orbits of comets. The problem of comets' motion was solved by Isaac Newton and his friend Edmond Halley (rhymes with "valley").

Halley to the Rescue

Newton's theory of gravity explained why the planets moved as Kepler described. Newton's friend, Edmond Halley, used Newton's theory to plot the orbits of comets. Halley saw that, while the orbits of most planets are nearly circular, the orbits of comets are long and narrow ellipses. When Halley plotted the orbits of the comets of 1682, 1607, and 1531, he discovered that their orbits were very similar. Halley guessed that the three comets must be one and the same.

Halley predicted that the comet of 1682 would return in 1758. He died 16 years before his forecast came true, but the comet whose return he predicted is known as Halley's Comet in honor of his success.

By the time Halley did his historic work, astronomers were using telescopes to discover more comets. One great comet-finder was Charles Messier (MESS-ee-AY). Messier kept a list of galaxies, star clusters, and nebulae that could be confused for faint comets. Though Messier considered himself mainly a comet-hunter (he discovered at least 15), modern amateur astronomers remember him for the *Messier Catalogue*. (The labels "M-1," "M-42," etc., on some objects in star charts mean that they are included in Messier's list.)

During the 1800s, Newton's theory was used to show that many comets were *periodic*, returning on regular, predictable schedules. Comets lost much of their power to inspire fear, and instead began to inspire the curiosity of astronomers who applied new methods and instruments to the study of these unusual objects.

Newton and Halley had helped to show that comets were not supernatural monsters, but celestial bodies obeying the same laws of nature as the planets. But that was only the first step in understanding these "hairy stars." Astronomers still had to figure out what comets are, and where they come from.

Every point on a circle is the same distance from the center or *focus*. An ellipse has two *foci* (FOE-sigh — that's the plural of focus). The two lines from any point on an ellipse to the foci add up to the same length as the lines from any other point. A circle is really a special kind of ellipse, one where the two foci are in the same spot.

CIRCLE

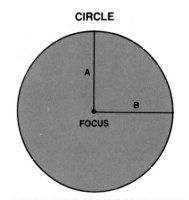

LINES A AND B ARE THE SAME LENGTH

ELLIPSE

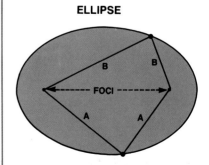

THE TOTAL LENGTH OF LINES A + A IS THE SAME AS THE TOTAL LENGTH OF LINES B + B

Continued on next page . . .

The best way to understand ellipses is to make some. You will need a sheet of corrugated cardboard (from an old box), two thumbtacks, some string, and a pencil.

Place the thumbtacks about 5 inches apart and press them into the cardboard. Don't press them in all the way; leave the heads a little above the surface.

Cut a piece of string about 12 inches long. Tie the ends together and loop it over the thumbtacks. Hook the pencil inside the loop and pull it as far away from the tacks as the string will allow. Keeping the string tight, draw a sweeping curve all the way around the tacks. As you draw, notice that the two sections of string running from the tacks to the pencil change length, but of course the combined length of the two sections remains the same (the section between the tacks never changes length).

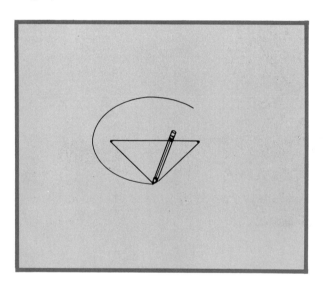

When you're done, you'll have a long, skinny oval.

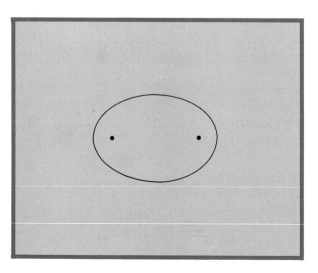

Draw another ellipse, but this time place the tacks only 2 inches apart. You will get a figure that looks almost like a circle.

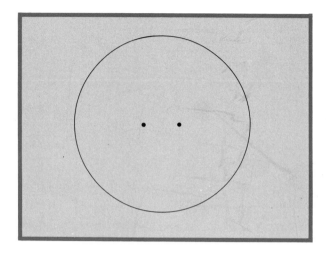

The tacks are the foci of your ellipses. The closer the foci are to one another, the more the ellipse resembles a circle. Remember, a circle is just an ellipse with the foci at the same spot. To prove this, draw a figure using just one tack — the same thing as having one tack on top of the other.

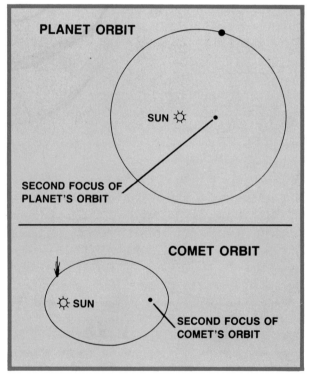

The orbits of planets and comets are ellipses with the Sun at one focus. The second focus of a planet's orbit is quite near the Sun; the second focus of a comet's orbit may be very far away. Planets' orbits are nearly circular and resemble the second ellipse you drew. Comets' orbits are long and skinny, like your first ellipse.

Chapter 2

What Is A Comet?

One of the brightest comets of the last 10 years, Comet West made a spectacular appearance in 1976.

Photo by Mark Erickson

People often think that the chance to see a comet comes once in a lifetime, but a bright, naked-eye comet appears roughly once every ten years. That's often enough to give anyone a chance to get a good look at several.

Suppose a friend just called to tell you that a comet is visible. Naturally, you go outside after supper to have a look. What can you expect to see?

In the dim glow of dusk you see a smudge of light. You thought it might be streaking through the sky like a shooting star, but it's just hanging there. You're not sure of its shape; it's not as clear as, say, the Moon. But your friend arrives with a pair of binoculars. Now you can see a "smoke puff." As the sky darkens, it's easier to see the familiar shape you've seen in pictures: the circular head and faint tail.

At an observatory hundreds of miles away, an astronomer has been watching the same comet for weeks. She discovered it accidentally in a photograph she took while searching for asteroids.

Back then, the comet was just a speck of light: no glowing head;

Astronomer/artist William K. Hartmann created this picture of the surface of a comet's nucleus.

© William K. Hartmann

no tail. The astronomer and her colleagues have been observing the comet carefully and taking measurements with sensitive detectors. As striking as the comet appears to your untrained eye, the astronomers have seen an even more amazing show: the growth of the comet from a dim, starlike point to the beautiful object you see tonight. To the scientists, comets are one of the most fascinating puzzles of the universe.

Most astronomers today think of comets as "dirty snowballs," chunks of ice and dust that spend most of their time in the farthest reaches of the Solar System. They are tiny — astronomers guess that the largest are about 50 miles across, and most are only 300 feet to 6 miles across. This small chunk, or *nucleus* (NEW-klee-uss), is the heart of a comet.

Far from the Sun, these small objects are nothing more than pinpoints of light in even the largest telescopes. Dark and dingy — like old snow on the side of a road — the nuclei (NEW-klee-eye: that's the plural of nucleus) feebly reflect the weak light from the distant Sun. At this distance, comets look nothing like the dramatic objects that have amazed humans for centuries. But as a comet nears the Sun, it goes through a spectacular change.

Presto Change-o

The transformation of a comet begins 3 to 5 AU from the Sun. (An AU, or *astronomical unit*, is the average distance of Earth from the Sun — about 93 million miles.) Solar radiation and the solar wind begin to heat the comet and strip off a thin outer layer. The ice in this layer *sublimates* — it turns directly into gas without becoming liquid in between, like dry ice (frozen carbon dioxide). Together with dust, the gas spreads into a huge *coma* (KOE-mah),

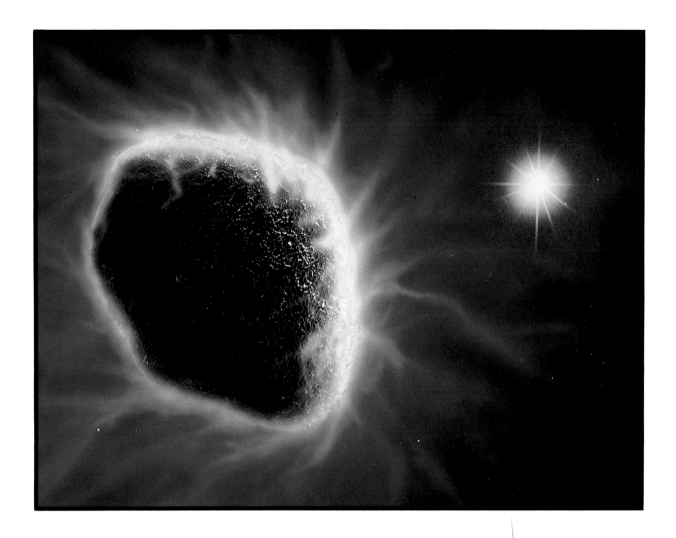

which can swell to hundreds of thousands of miles across.

Comets that have made several trips around the Sun often have a coating of dust. As sunlight heats this outer dust shell, some of the sublimated ice beneath shoots out in a jet of gas, and the dust is forced out into the coma. These jets often change the course of a comet slightly, which explains why predictions of comet returns may be a day or two off.

Sunlight causes the gas in the coma to glow, much the way electricity flowing through a fluorescent tube creates light. Some additional light is contributed by the reflection of sunlight from the dust particles.

Astronomers recently discovered that the bright coma is surrounded by an even larger cloud of hydrogen. This cloud is invisible from Earth, but has been detected by spacecraft carrying instruments sensitive to ultraviolet radiation.

The nucleus is now hidden within the huge glowing coma. The faint, tiny body has wrapped itself in a glowing cloud many times larger than Earth. But this doesn't complete the transformation, for the comet has also been sprouting a tail.

Because many of the bright, well-known comets seen throughout history have tails, it's hard to picture a comet without one. In fact, most comets discovered by modern astronomers develop only faint tails that cannot be seen with the naked eye. Astronomers have found two kinds of tails: dust tails and gas tails. Dust tails usually develop first, forming when the comet is 3 to 5 AU from the Sun. They are made up mainly of the dust that

Still invisible from Earth, a comet begins to respond to the warmth of the distant Sun.

Painting by John Foster

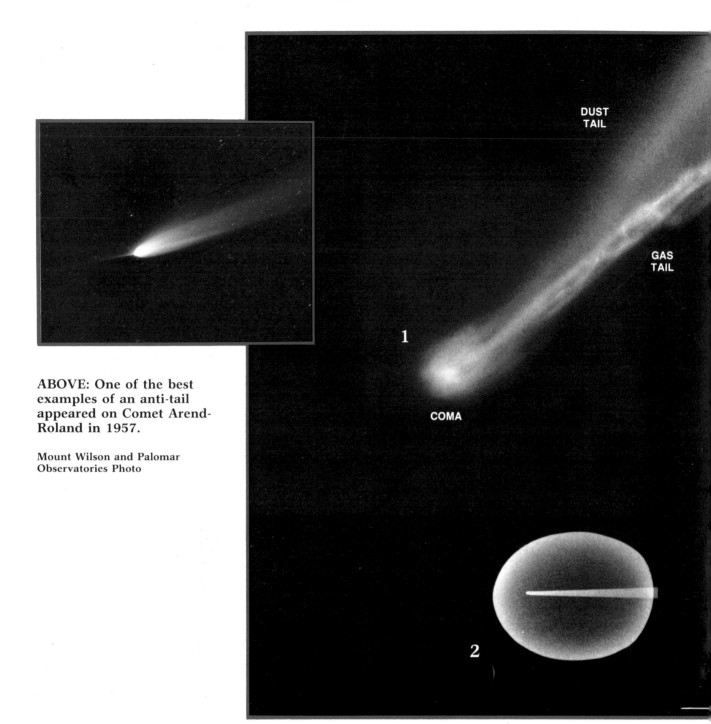

DUST
TAIL

GAS
TAIL

1

COMA

2

ABOVE: One of the best examples of an anti-tail appeared on Comet Arend-Roland in 1957.

Mount Wilson and Palomar Observatories Photo

1. The parts of a comet. The coma, which completely hides the nucleus, is trailed by a knotty gas tail (lower) and smoother, gently curving dust tail (upper).

2. The hydrogen cloud is a huge, invisible halo surrounding the comet.

3. A comet's tail, blown by the solar wind, always points away from the Sun.

Art by Thomas L. Hunt

is freed when the comet's ice turns to vapor, and shine with reflected sunlight. The curving dust tails can stretch millions of miles beyond the comet.

The gas tails usually develop within 2 AU of the Sun. Gas tails are straighter than dust tails, and can stretch ten times farther from the comet. These gassy tails often contain clumps or swirling knots of material, and these details can change dramatically in only a few hours. Like the coma, gas tails emit their own light.

Comets can have several dust tails and a gas tail at the same time, or one kind and not the other. Because they are created by the pressure of solar radiation and the solar wind, the tails generally point away from the Sun, trailing behind on the way in, but leading on the way out. Every so often, a comet will develop an "anti-tail," which appears to travel *in front* of the

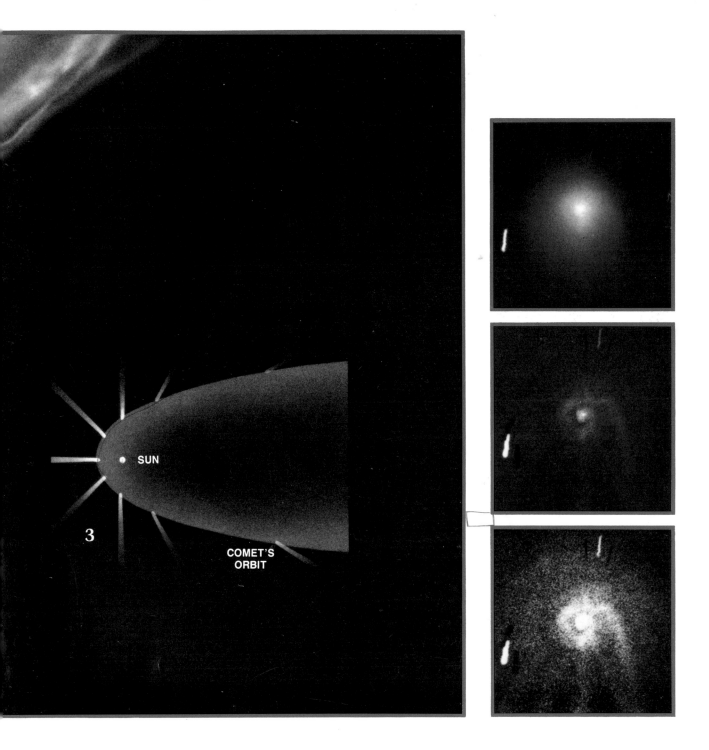

SUN

3

COMET'S
ORBIT

comet. Astronomers think that this is only an optical illusion caused by our point of view from Earth.

The Mysterious Nucleus

The study of comets is basically a process of observing comas and tails, then trying to guess the nature of the nuclei they spring from. The problem is that comet nuclei are just dim points of light when far from the Sun, and hidden by the coma when they are nearer. No one has been able to measure a comet's nucleus accurately, and they aren't massive enough to "weigh" by the usual methods. Without knowing the size and mass, we can't tell a nucleus' *density*, which is an important clue to what it's made of. So most of what we know about comet nuclei has been learned indirectly, by studying the comas and tails they create.

ABOVE: New views of an old comet. The top photo is a plate taken of Comet Halley in 1910. Below it are two image processed photos of the same plate, showing jets. The curve of the jets shows the spin of the nucleus.

Mount Wilson Observatory Photo processed at the Lunar and Planetary Lab, University of Arizona

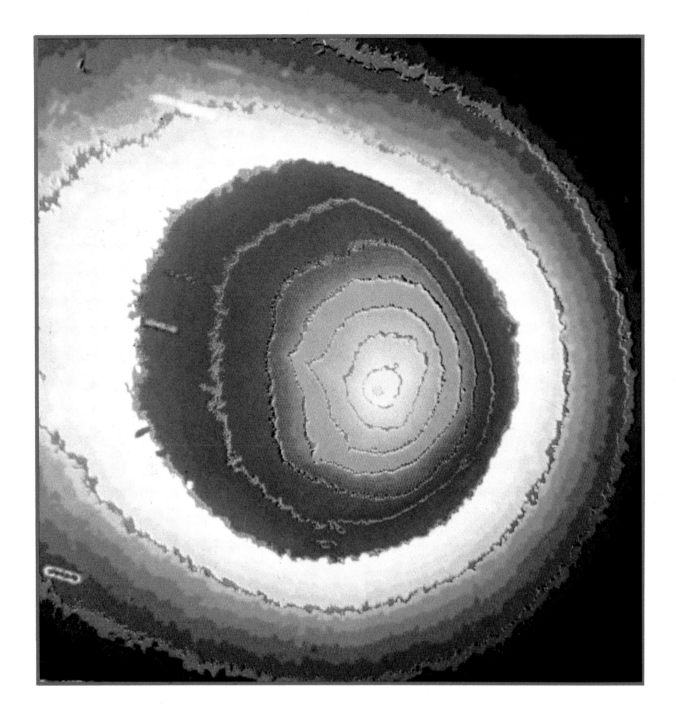

Modern image processing techniques recover invisible structure in old photos. This image is the result of reprocessing a photo of Halley's Comet taken from Egypt in 1910.

NASA photo courtesy D. Klinglesmith, Goddard Space Flight Center

Scientists know that the gasses in the coma are not the same as the material in the comet — sunlight has changed the original ices. But astronomers can guess what chemicals these gasses come from. The invisible hydrogen cloud is strong evidence that comets contain water. They probably also contain methane and ammonia. And we know that they contain some dust.

But how much ice, how much dust? No one really knows for sure. A few astronomers suspect that comets are not really dirty snowballs at all, but rocky objects covered by a layer of dust and ice. There is still a lot to be learned about what lies at the heart of a comet, and what makes it tick.

Knowing what comets are made of could give us important clues to how they were formed and where they came from. But it might be possible to go the other way around: If we could learn how and where comets were formed, perhaps we could figure out their composition.

Chapter 3

Where Do Comets Come From?

In the cold depths of space, an unexpected guest is making its way toward a distant bright star. It had spent millions of years circling the star, like an invisible moth circling a light. But gravity, not light, is what attracts this silent traveler, and a chance nudge from even deeper space has altered its destiny forever.

Three million years ago, its path was changed to a near-collision course with the star. In a year or so, the icy visitor will be "turned on" by the star's heat. When the star is a huge, blazing sun, eyes on the third planet will turn toward the new arrival, gazing upon it for the first time . . .

Tracing Comets

Each year, astronomers find about 10 comets. Half of these are comets that have been seen at least once before, and are returning as expected. The rest are "surprises," some making their first appearances to human eyes. Where are these comets coming from?

To understand a comet's origin, astronomers first have to find its path in space. Astronomers need only a few good observations to compute the size and shape of a comet's orbit and determine the orbit's location in space. Next, they study how the gravity of the planets may have changed the comet's course. When all the calculations are done, astronomers are able to tell when and

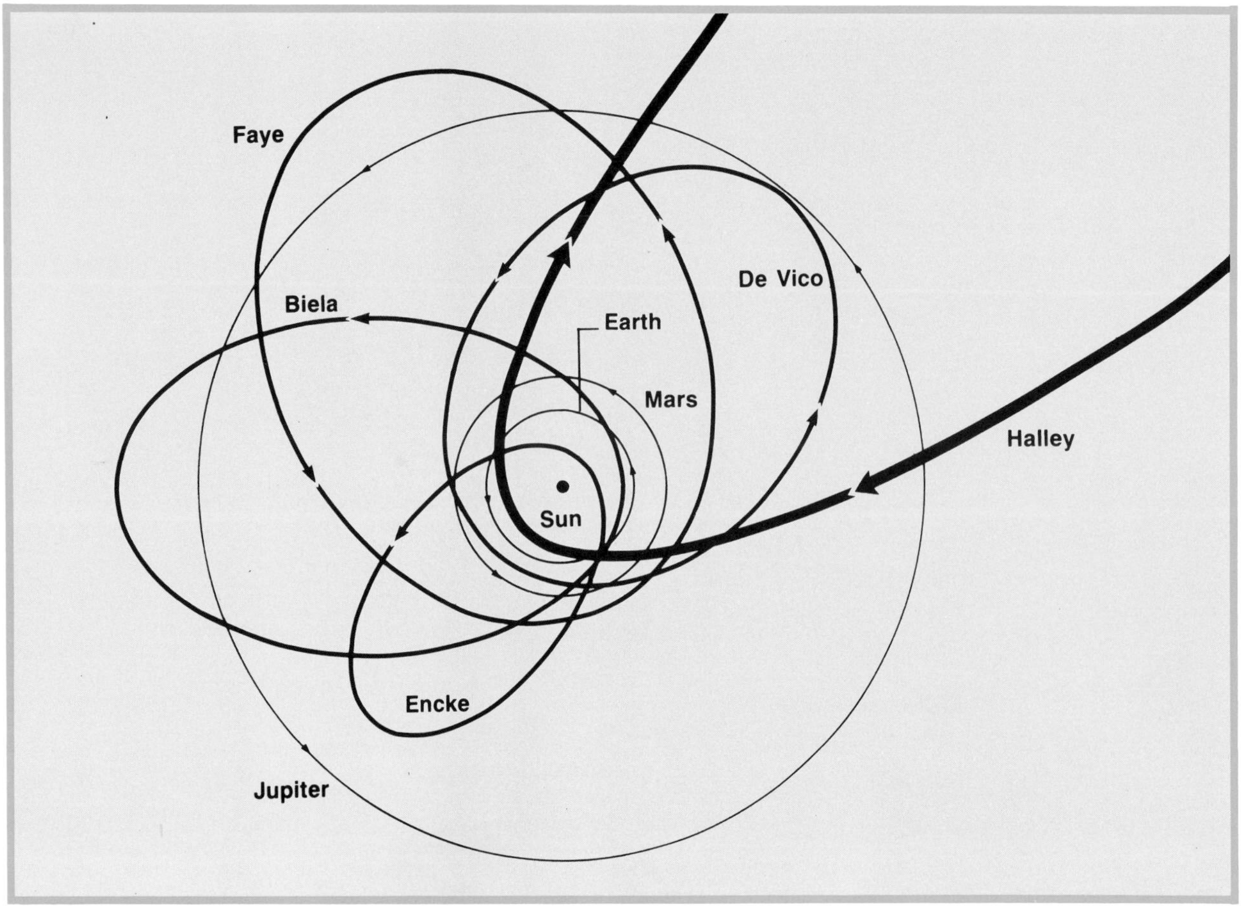
Faye
Biela
De Vico
Earth
Mars
Halley
Sun
Encke
Jupiter

A sampling of some short-period comet orbits. Members of the "Jupiter family" don't stray much beyond that giant planet, and move in the same direction as the planets. Comet Halley, on the other hand, is a short-period comet that travels far beyond Jupiter with a retrograde orbit that carries it in a direction opposite that of the planets.

where the comet will be at *perihelion* (pair-ih-HEE-lee-un) and *aphelion* (ap-HEE-lee-un) — its closest and farthest points from the Sun. They also know the comet's *period*, the time it takes to complete one orbit.

Astronomers divide comets into two groups, according to their orbits: short-period comets and long-period comets. Short-period comets take less than 200 years to orbit the Sun; long-period comets take 200 years or more — up to millions of years.

Short-period comets tend to be fainter than long-period ones. This is simply because they have made more passages near the Sun, and much of the material that forms the bright tails and comas has been lost during earlier trips.

Another feature of short-period comets is that they generally travel in the same direction as the planets, counter-clockwise as seen from above the Sun. (Astronomers call this *direct* or *prograde* motion; *retrograde* motion carries an object in a clockwise direction.) Short-period comets also remain close to the *plane of the ecliptic*, the imaginary flat disk which the planets' orbits lie on.

Calculations show that short-period comets began their careers as long-period comets: Their orbits have been altered by the planets' gravity. Each time a comet passes through the region of the planets, its orbit can be changed by the pull of the planets. Eventually, a comet can be "captured" into a short-period orbit.

Jupiter has the strongest gravity of all the planets, and most short-period comets travel no farther from the Sun than about 5 AU — roughly Jupiter's distance from the Sun. In fact, Jupiter has its own family of comets, the *Jupiter family*.

So short-period comets come from long-period comets. But

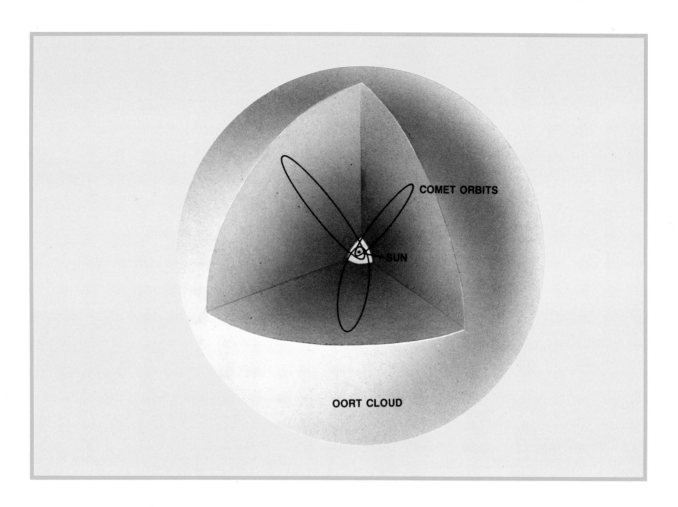

COMET ORBITS

SUN

OORT CLOUD

where do long-period comets come from?

Let's look at the clues we have to work with. First, we've seen that comets probably contain water, methane, ammonia, other ices, and dust. The same ingredients are found between the stars, in interstellar clouds. Second, unlike the planets and short-period comets, long-period comets can travel high above or below the ecliptic — they come from all directions — and they can have either direct or retrograde orbits. Third, calculations show that comets are members of the Solar System — they orbit the Sun.

A successful theory of the origin of comets must explain why they belong to the Sun's family, yet resemble interstellar matter.

Early astronomers thought comets could be interstellar "junk" caught by the Sun as it orbits the galaxy. That would explain comets' resemblance to interstellar clouds. But this idea won't work: Most interstellar comets could not be permanently captured by the Sun. They would head back out into interstellar space after one encounter with the Sun, never to return. Astronomers have never seen a comet with an orbit that will take it into interstellar space — all comets are members of the Solar System.

The Oort Cloud

In 1950, Jan Oort studied the orbits of 19 long-period comets and concluded that "new" comets (those making their first trip near the Sun and planets) come from a huge cloud that surrounds the Sun. Later studies supported Oort's theory, and the existence of this *Oort Cloud* is widely accepted among astronomers.

Oort's theory explains why we discover about five new comets each year. The Oort Cloud starts 20,000 AU from the Sun, and

Long-period comets appear to come from the Oort Cloud, a hollow sphere extending 20,000 to about 200,000 AU from the Sun. The white area represents the space within the inner limits of the Oort Cloud; the black dot at the center is the Sun. Comets enter the region of the planets (too small to be seen on this scale) from all parts of the Oort Cloud.

Dust still fills the Solar System as the Sun's nuclear "fire" ignites, illuminating a still-forming gas giant planet.

Painting by Mark Paternostro

extends to 200,000 AU. At this distance, the gravity of passing stars is nearly as important as the Sun's gravity. Comets can be "bumped" by the gravity of other stars, causing about 200 to enter the region of the planets each year. We see only the five or so that are near and bright enough to be visible from Earth. The passing stars come from all directions, so comets from all parts of the cloud can be bumped toward the Sun. This explains why comets come from all directions and have both direct and retrograde orbits.

Okay, so comets come from the Oort Cloud. Now, where did the Oort Cloud come from? To answer this question, astronomers look back to the early days of the Solar System.

Astronomers believe that the Sun and planets formed from a huge interstellar cloud. As this cloud, or *nebula*, collapsed, it flattened into a disk. Most of the material wound up in a ball at the center of the disk. Bits of dust and gas in the disk collided and stuck together, becoming larger and larger chunks called *planetesimals* (plan-eh-TESS-ih-mulls). A few clumps grew big enough for their gravity to pull smaller planetesimals toward them, which made them grow faster than the rest. The central mass became our Sun, and the largest clumps became the planets. Astronomers believe that the area of the disk inside Jupiter was too hot for ices and gasses to collect into planets; that's why the inner planets — from Mercury to Mars — are rocky objects, while the outer planets are mainly gas giants surrounded by icy moons.

How does the Oort Cloud fit into this picture?

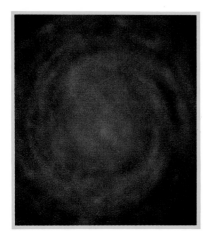  

Filling the Oort Cloud

It's not likely that the comets formed where the Oort Cloud is now. Most astronomers think that this farthest region of the Solar System never contained enough material to form the million million or so comets thought to exist in the Oort Cloud.

The most widely accepted theory holds that comets are leftovers of the formation of the planets Uranus and Neptune.

While the large planets were growing, their gravity pulled more and more material toward them. As they got close to their present sizes, however, the planets could also give small planetesimals a gravitational "kick." With their orbits "pumped up," some planetesimals (or "cometesimals") would travel far from the orbits of the planets.

The largest planets, Jupiter and Saturn, give big kicks; only a few percent of the comets they threw out would have ended up in the Oort Cloud — most would have left the Solar System completely. Uranus and Neptune, however, are smaller, and a much higher percent of the comets they ejected could have wound up in the Oort Cloud.

But some astronomers suspect that this part of the Solar System was too warm for icy comets to form there. Others think that, while Uranus and Neptune could have thrown *some* comets into the Oort Cloud, their gravitational "aim" wouldn't have been good enough to put a million million comets into the cloud.

There is still another possibility. While there are no known planets beyond 40 AU, the original disk of the Solar System probably reached as far as 5,000 AU. In 1981, astronomer Jack

A bird's-eye view of the birth of the Solar System. The pictures on this page show the stages of planetary formation from the collapse of the nebula (top left) to today's arrangement of planets (lower right).

Artwork by Victor Costanzo

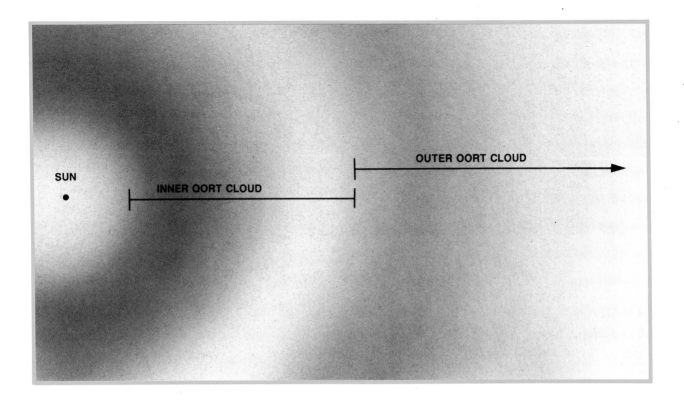

INNER OORT CLOUD

OUTER OORT CLOUD

SUN

Some astronomers suspect that, in addition to the million million comets within the Oort Cloud, there may be a hundred times that many in an inner cloud. The inner edge of the nearer cloud may lie about 3,000 AU from the Sun. The comets of the inner cloud rarely get pushed into the region of the planets.

Hills proposed that there may be an *inner Oort Cloud* that holds up to a hundred times more comets than the outer cloud. These comets would have formed about 3,000 AU from the Sun, over 70 times farther away than the most distant known planet. We only see comets from the outer cloud, because the inner comets usually aren't "bumped" by distant stars.

The Oort Cloud fits nicely into this theory. Every 500 million years or so, a star could pass close enough to the Sun to affect members of the inner cloud. Since there are a lot more comets in the inner cloud, the result of this gravitational nudge would be a "shower" of thousands of comets falling into the region of the planets. Many of these comets would be destroyed, or knocked out of the Solar System by gravitational "kicks" from the large planets. But many comets would be redirected into the outer Oort Cloud. Once in the outer cloud, the comets would be bumped toward the planets by passing stars, as Oort described.

The major problem with this theory is that scientists are not sure that comets could have formed as far from the Sun as the inner cloud would be. Yet if the Solar System's original disk stretched as far as 5,000 AU, it's easy to suspect that this region isn't as empty as people have assumed.

There is no perfect theory on how comets formed, but the Oort Cloud accounts for the strange orbits of comets. And if comets formed in the earliest days of the Solar System, it would make sense for them to resemble interstellar clouds — that's what the Sun and planets formed from in the first place.

Whether comets formed around Uranus and Neptune or somewhere beyond the planets, we have discovered another reason to study comets: They may be pure samples of the nebula that gave birth to the Solar System. These visitors from deep space may also be visitors from the past, with secrets to tell about the birth of our Sun, our planet, and other familiar members of our Solar System.

Chapter 4

Do Comets Affect Earth?

A comet passes near the Earth and Moon. Scientists are exploring the possibility that comets mean more to Earth than just a pretty sight.

Painting by Mark Paternostro

By 1910, educated people knew that comets were as natural as the planets, not evil demons or signs of disaster. Yet when people heard that Earth was going to pass through the tail of Halley's Comet, there was a minor panic.

At least the fear wasn't superstitious this time. After all, scientists had learned that comet tails contained the poisonous gas cyanogen (a cousin of cyanide). Worried people bought "comet pills" and "inhalers" designed to filter out the dangerous gas.

They wasted their money. In the first place, at the closest encounter there was about one molecule of comet gas for every 10 billion molecules of air! Besides, nearly all the material from the comet remained trapped in the upper atmosphere, unable to reach the surface of the Earth.

Is there any way that comets affect us?

From "Hairy Stars" to "Shooting Stars"

Meteor showers are a pleasant side effect of comets. If you go out on an average moonless night, you can expect to see about eight meteors (or "shooting stars") per hour streaking through every part of the sky. Several times a year, however, stargazers are treated to a *meteor shower*. During such a shower, you'll see as many as 50 meteors per hour coming from a particular spot in the sky, called the *radiant*. A meteor shower is named after

Photo by Allan E. Morton

Meteor Crater in Arizona. This ¾-mile-diameter crater was created by a meteorite impact 50,000 years ago.

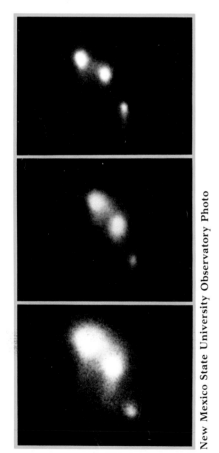

New Mexico State University Observatory Photo

Comet West breaks apart after passing perihelion.

the constellation in which its radiant lies. Each meteor shower occurs about the same time each year. The *Perseid* shower, whose radiant lies in the constellation Perseus, occurs every year around August 12. (See ''Looking for Meteors'' for more about meteor showers and how to enjoy them.)

Meteors are glowing bits of ''space junk'' streaking through Earth's atmosphere. Outer space is full of bits of rock and dust called *meteoroids*. Our planet constantly sweeps up this material as it travels along its orbit. Meteoroids travel at thousands of miles an hour, and friction with molecules of air heats them until they become glowing meteors. (Most meteors are destroyed by the heat; those few that reach the surface of Earth are called *meteorites*.)

During the 19th century, astronomers realized that showers occur when Earth passes through concentrations of debris called *meteor streams*. When they studied the orbits of these meteor streams, astronomers saw that many streams follow the paths of known comets.

The orbits of comets are littered with fluffy bits of dust that are stripped from the comet nucleus. Whenever the Earth passes through a comet's orbit, our planet's atmosphere sweeps up millions of bits of this cosmic dust.

Meteor streams may bring more than a lively display, however. Many scientists are convinced that the great 1908 explosion near the Tunguska River in Siberia was the result of a collision with a large chunk of comet. One astronomer has suggested that the object was a member of the meteoroid stream that gives us the Beta Taurid meteor shower every June. This would make the object a piece of Encke's Comet, whose litter creates the Beta Taurid shower.

Most astronomers think such collisions are rare, occurring perhaps once every 2,000 years. But some recent theories suggest that collisions might occur more frequently.

Showers in the Forecast?

Jack Hills, the astronomer who suggested that there is an inner Oort Cloud containing 100 million million comets, also looked into what such a cloud might mean to Earth. He has calculated that, on the average, a star could pass through the inner cloud every 500 million years or so. The result would be a disastrous "comet shower."

A comet shower might last about 700,000 years. Ten thousand comets would enter the region of the planets every year — instead of the usual 200. Ten to 200 comets could strike the Earth during one of these showers. What might such a bombardment mean to Earth?

One of the great puzzles of Earth's ancient history is the sudden disappearance of the dinosaurs about 65 million years ago. Lately, some scientists have wondered whether their extinction might have an extraterrestrial cause. For example, if an asteroid collided with Earth, the dust lifted into the atmosphere could block sunlight, cooling our planet. A change in temperature could affect plant life, perhaps wiping out the food supply for some animals — like the dinosaurs.

Geologists have studied soil and rock deposits that were laid around the time the dinosaurs disappeared. They have found that the element iridium is present in greater amounts than are normally found on Earth. Extraterrestrial objects like asteroids contain a lot of iridium. The dust thrown into the atmosphere

Some scientists suspect that a comet shower may have caused the disappearance of the dinosaurs 65 million years ago.

Painting by Mark Paternostro

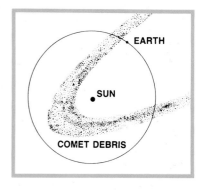

When Earth enters the stream of debris left by a comet, bits of matter enter the atmosphere to burn up and become meteors.

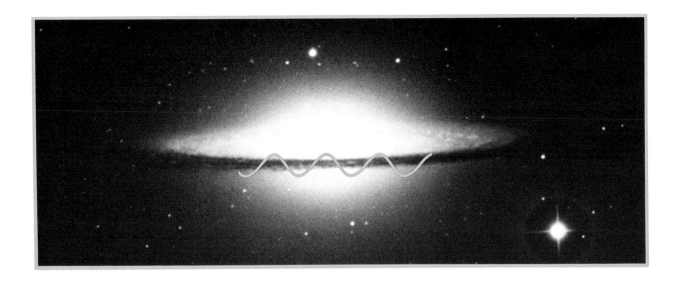

Gas and dust are concentrated in the plane of some galaxies, like M-104 above. The Sun's wavy orbit takes us through the plane of the Milky Way galaxy every 33 million years. Collisions with gas clouds in the plane might create comet showers.

Hale Observatories Photo

by the impact of an extraterrestrial object would settle into a layer rich in iridium.

A comet shower might have the same effect as a collision with a large asteroid.

This possibility leads us to other far out theories connecting comets to undiscovered members of the Solar System.

Some scientists have suggested that there is a pattern of earthly disasters with extraterrestrial causes. In 1983, two scientists suggested that whole species of plants and animals are wiped out every 26 million years or so. And some geologists who have studied the ages of craters on Earth think that the Earth is bombarded on a regular schedule. We've already seen how such bombardment might cause the disappearance of certain life forms.

Three Ways to Make a Shower

Astronomers have quickly come up with three theories to explain periodic disasters.

The first theory involves the way the Sun orbits in the Milky Way galaxy. It so happens that the Sun's orbit is "wavy," and our star passes through the plane of the galaxy roughly every 33 million years. The galaxy's gravitational forces are strongest in the plane, and it's possible that the extra gravity could give the Oort Cloud enough of a nudge to cause a comet shower. A collision with an interstellar cloud could cause a shower, too. Interstellar clouds are more numerous near the plane, and some astronomers expect shower-causing collisions near the plane crossing.

One problem with this theory is that the Sun last passed through the plane about 11 million years ago, but there is no evidence that a mass extinction occurred then. Another problem is that this pattern is roughly 7 million years out of step with the extinction pattern. And some astronomers think that collisions with clouds are as likely to happen above or below the plane as at the plane itself. That would rule out interstellar clouds as a cause of periodic showers.

The second idea is that the Sun is part of a double star system, with a small dark companion (nicknamed "Nemesis") completing a long, thin orbit every 26 million years or so. If its orbit takes it close enough to the Oort Cloud (or to Jack Hills' inner cloud),

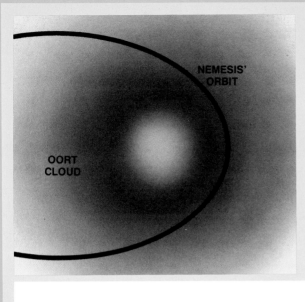

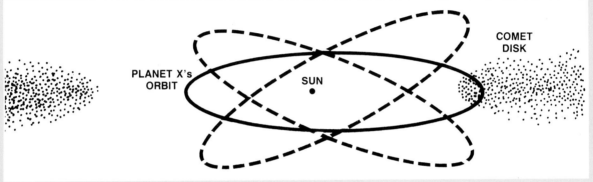

LEFT: Nemesis, the Sun's proposed faint companion star, could have a long, thin orbit. Its closest approach to the Sun might take Nemesis through the Oort Cloud, creating a comet shower.

BELOW: For Planet X to cause comet showers, it would have to have a wobbling orbit that could take it through a disk (not a cloud) of comets beyond Neptune's orbit. According to the theory, Planet X would usually lie above the disk, or within a zone free of comets. Every 26 million years or so, however, the planet could reach aphelion inside the disk, knocking loose a shower of comets.

it could provide a gravitational "bump" to thousands of comets, creating a shower on a regular schedule.

No one has seen Nemesis, though the search has just begun. It may never be found, even if it does exist. Over billions of years, the gravity of passing stars, and of the galaxy itself, might have caused Nemesis' orbit to grow larger and larger. Nemesis may have already escaped the Sun's gravity to wander through the galaxy on its own.

The third idea suggests that "Planet X" is the culprit. The orbits of the outer planets Uranus and Neptune are slightly unpredictable. The simplest explanation is that the planets are being tugged at by the gravity of an unseen planet, often called Planet X. Pluto was discovered during a search for such a planet, but Pluto isn't massive enough to affect Uranus and Neptune. Could a large planet beyond Neptune explain the odd planetary motions *and* cause comet showers?

Probably not. The main problem is that, while Planet X could knock comets toward the other planets, it couldn't produce the sharp burst of comets needed for a periodic comet shower.

Some scientists don't buy the theories of extraterrestrial catastrophes. An unusual amount of volcanic activity could have the same effect on Earth's climate as a collision with a comet or asteroid. It might even explain the high iridium levels: High levels of iridium have been found in lava flowing from volcanoes. Of course, it's also possible that a comet shower could trigger a sudden increase in volcanic eruptions!

Collision! Every day, our planet sweeps up tons of space dust, which floats gently to Earth. Sometimes, though, a large object — a comet, large meteorite, or asteroid — strikes the Earth. The impact of one or more large chunks of cosmic debris might affect the history of life on our planet.

Painting by Adolf Schaller

Comets and Life?

There is an even more spectacular theory on how comets could have affected Earth's history — by bringing life here in the first place! Many of the chemicals necessary for life are found in comets. Two scientists, Fred Hoyle and Chandra Wickramasinghe, believe comets could be the birthplace of primitive life forms. They think comets could bring life to planets they collide with.

Current evidence does not rule out the theory. But while simple organic molecules exist in comets, the more complex ones that lead to life probably don't form in these icy objects. Besides the absence of liquid water in space, there is a lot of radiation which could destroy complex molecules, as well as life itself.

Even if life within a comet could have survived the violent trip to Earth, it seems unlikely that it could have endured the change of environment; it's hard to imagine an earthly life form surviving a move to the inside of a comet!

* * *

Comets are no longer frightening — but they certainly are puzzling. What are they? Small chunks of ice and a bit of dust — we think. Where do they come from? From the Oort Cloud — we think. How, when, and where were they formed? Somewhere around Uranus and Neptune during the birth of the Solar System — possibly.

As we've seen, trying to figure out comets is like trying to assemble a jigsaw puzzle without all the pieces. Parts of the puzzle have been assembled in ways that convince many astronomers. But some astronomers have found it possible to arrange the pieces in several different ways, and no section of the puzzle is considered complete. Who knows what the picture will look like when all the pieces have been found?

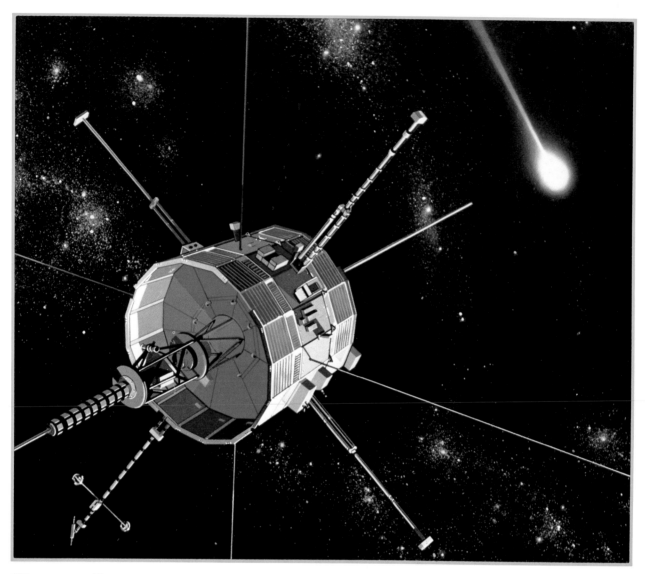

Chapter 5

The Halley Missions

From the days of Edmond Halley through much of the 19th century, most of what we thought about comets came from the study of their motions. Later, as physicists learned more about the way radiation is created and reflected by atoms, the light from comets was carefully analyzed to reveal more about what these mysterious objects are made of, and where they come from. Learning about comets has been a slow, difficult process.

But we are about to enjoy an explosion of information about comets. The key to this burst of knowledge is our ability to reach into space to examine comets close up. Five spacecraft are being sent to greet Halley's Comet. The pictures and data they send to Earth will probably tell us more in two weeks than we've learned in the past 20 years.

Why spend millions of dollars to send probes to a comet? And

ICE, the International Cometary Explorer, was sent to encounter Comet Giacobini-Zinner (jah-coh-BEE-nee ZIN-ner), making it the first spacecraft to meet a comet. Besides its important investigations of Giacobini-Zinner, ICE will contribute information useful to the Halley intercept missions.

NASA Art

Pioneer Venus will be on the same side of the Sun as Halley when the comet reaches perihelion. For about eight weeks before, during, and after perihelion, the spacecraft will measure the ultraviolet light from the comet, providing information on the gasses in the coma and the amounts of gas and dust emitted by the comet.

NASA Art

why Halley's Comet? First of all, scientists think that comets are pure samples of the materials that formed the Sun and planets. They hold important evidence from the earliest history of the Solar System. Second, our atmosphere limits what we can learn with Earth-based instruments. There's a lot going on that we just can't see from Earth; the spacecraft will give us the closer look we need to learn more about comets.

Halley's Comet is a good target for our spacecraft. Comets that have made many orbits around the Sun are "burned out": Solar radiation has changed them, and they can't tell us much about "pure" comets. Comets making their first trips near the Sun would be the best to study, but we never have enough warning to prepare a mission. Halley's Comet is a good compromise: It is a bright comet, which means it is relatively "young," and so roughly resembles comets that have never been near the Sun. Plus, its orbit is well known, making it a lot easier to "aim" a spacecraft for an intercept mission.

One of the great disappointments of the Space Age was the failure of the United States to send a sophisticated probe to study Halley's Comet. But the American space program will still make some useful contributions to the international scientific effort to take advantage of Halley's return.

The U.S. Effort

In August 1978, the third International Sun-Earth Explorer, ISEE-3, was launched to study the way Earth's magnetic field is affected by the stream of particles that makes up the solar wind. After spending four years between the Earth and the Sun, ISEE-3 was maneuvered to swing through the opposite end of Earth's

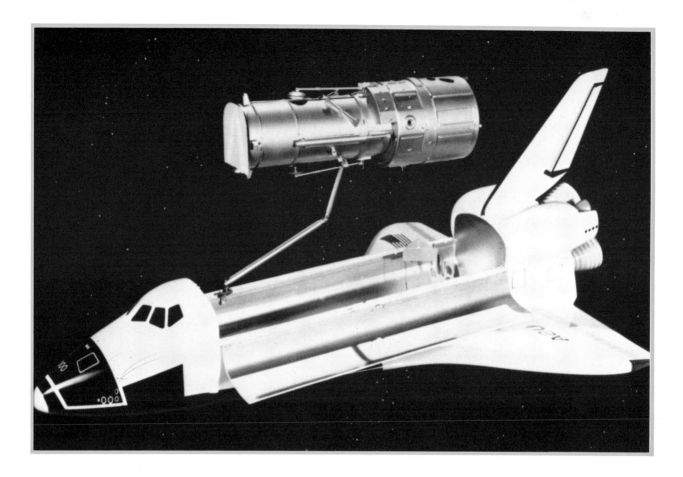

magnetosphere, the long magnetotail. Mission planners then realized that it would be possible to send the craft through a different kind of tail — the gas tail of the comet Giacobini-Zinner.

Once on its way to the comet, ISEE-3 was officially renamed the International Cometary Explorer, or ICE. Its scheduled meeting with Giacobini-Zinner in September 1985 makes ICE the first probe to encounter a comet.

After passing through Giacobini-Zinner's tail, ICE's path will twice bring it to positions "upwind" of Comet Halley. From these locations, ICE will be able to provide data on the solar wind *before* it reaches Halley. This will give scientists a better understanding of how the solar wind causes the effects other probes will observe.

Other U.S. space hardware will also be used to study Halley. The Solar Max satellite, repaired by a Shuttle crew in April 1984, was built to study the Sun. Its instruments will be able to provide images of the comet when it is too close to the Sun to be seen with most other equipment. Pioneer Venus, which has been orbiting Venus since 1978, will be on the far side of the Sun at the same time as Halley's Comet. This spacecraft will keep tabs on the comet when it is invisible from Earth.

The Shuttle will also get into the act. It will carry a package of ultraviolet cameras and wide-field telescopes to observe Comet Halley from low Earth orbit at the same time that five probes are making their closest approaches to the comet. In late January 1986, the Shuttle will deploy the Spartan Halley Mission satellite, which will orbit free of the Shuttle for 48 hours, then be retrieved by the Shuttle. Spartan will identify the chemicals being released by the comet during the very active period just before perihelion. Like Solar Max, Spartan is designed to observe the comet when

The Hubble Space Telescope, scheduled to be placed in orbit in August 1986, will enable astronomers to observe Halley at any time — even at aphelion, when the comet is farthest from the Sun.

NASA Photo

Planet-A, the Japanese Halley probe, will make the most distant approach of all the Halley intercept missions. Traveling to within about 100,000 miles of Halley, Planet-A will take ultraviolet pictures of the comet.

Painting by Mark Paternostro

it is very close to the Sun. Finally, once the Shuttle deploys the Hubble Space Telescope in the summer of 1986, we will never lose sight of Halley again. Scientists will be able to observe the comet whenever they like, even at its farthest distance from the Sun.

While the U.S. is making the most of its available hardware, the most important contributions to understanding Halley's Comet will be made by the five spacecraft that will be sent by other space agencies. Though launched up to eight months apart, they should all encounter the comet within eight days of one another in March 1986. From distances of 300 to about 9 million miles, the five probes will reveal many secrets about Halley's composition, and will carefully study the processes that make the glowing coma and tails. With luck, their data will include the first high-quality pictures of a comet's nucleus.

The Japanese Probes

Japan's space agency, the Institute of Space and Astronomical Sciences (ISAS), has prepared two probes to visit Comet Halley, MS-T5 and Planet-A. The probes are identical in design, but carry different scientific instruments. MS-T5 was originally designed only to test the equipment used on Planet-A, but some scientific instruments have been added. Like ICE, it will make measurements of interplanetary space far from the comet. It will

lie about 9 million miles from the comet when Planet-A makes its closest approach. Later, MS-T5 may be sent through the comet's tail about 600,000 miles from the nucleus.

Scheduled for launch in August 1985, Planet-A's main mission is to take ultraviolet pictures of Halley. This will provide information on the huge hydrogen cloud surrounding the comet. Together with MS-T5, Planet-A will also take measurements of the solar wind. Planet-A's closest approach will be about 100,000 miles from the comet on March 8.

ESA'S Giotto is scheduled to make the closest approach to Halley, within about 300 miles. If all goes well, it could provide us with the first closeup pictures of a comet's nucleus.

Painting by Mark Paternostro

The Soviet Vegas

The U.S.S.R.'s plans are probably the most ambitious. Not only will the Soviet Union send two probes to intercept Halley, but each craft has already visited Venus to deploy two probes there! (The name Vega comes from the first two letters of *Venera* and *Galley*, the Russian words for Venus and Halley.)

Vega 1 was launched on December 15, 1984. As it flew past Venus on June 11, 1985, it released a module containing an atmospheric probe and soft lander. The comet probe continued on its way toward a March 6, 1986, encounter with Halley. Vega 2 was launched on December 21, 1984. It released its Venus probes on June 15, 1985, and should arrive at Halley's Comet within a few days of Vega 1.

The Vegas will travel to within about 6,000 miles of the comet's

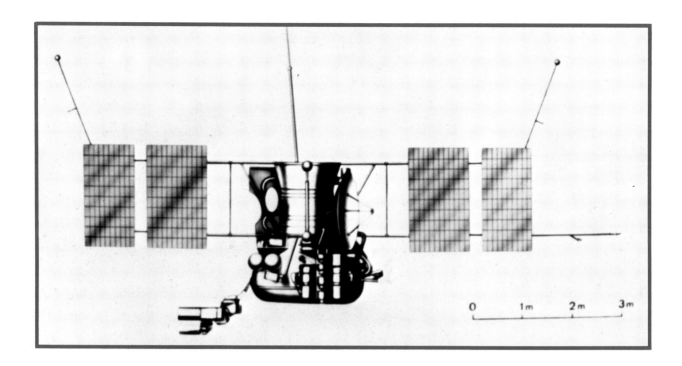

0   1 m   2 m   3 m

The Soviet Union is sending two identical Vega spacecraft to intercept Comet Halley. If the first Vega accomplishes its mission, the second may be sent much closer to the nucleus than the planned 6,000 miles.

Courtesy Vega Project

nucleus. There they will study the coma of gas and dust that surrounds the nucleus. The Soviet craft are the largest of the comet probes, each carrying 14 instruments from nine countries. Among the instruments are two cameras. One of these cameras should be able to see features 650 feet across on the nucleus. Because they have two craft, the Soviets may decide to send one closer than the planned 6,000 miles.

The Vegas need special protection for their trip inside the coma, a region filled with dust. The spacecraft will be traveling at high speeds, and collisions with billions of dust particles could cause serious damage. The shields protecting the craft will carry detectors to make measurements of the dust particles that strike them.

As we saw earlier, comets often create jets of dust that change their courses slightly. Halley is no exception, so data from the Vegas will be needed to plot the nucleus' position precisely. This information will be used for the mission that is making the closest planned approach to Comet Halley, Giotto.

Giotto

The European Space Agency (ESA) is sending the most advanced of all the comet probes, Giotto (JOT-toh). The spacecraft is named after the Italian artist who included an accurate representation of Halley's Comet in his painting, "The Adoration of the Magi." (The painting appears on page 8.)

Giotto is scheduled to make its closest approach on March 13, 1986. The Vegas, scheduled to arrive several days ahead of Giotto, will pinpoint Halley's nucleus, allowing Giotto's controllers to make last-minute course corrections.

ESA will try to send Giotto within about 300 miles of the nucleus. This region is even dustier than the area to be entered by the Vegas, and since the comet and Giotto are traveling roughly toward each other, the spacecraft will zoom through the dust at over 150,000 miles per hour! Giotto needs even more protection than the Vegas.

Two special shields will face the dust, protecting most of the spacecraft's 10 instruments, as well as the craft itself. Giotto's color camera will peek out from behind the shields like a periscope, preventing the dust from damaging the sensitive detectors. And since the solar panels will probably be "sand-blasted," Giotto carries four batteries to power it through the closest encounter.

Giotto's communications systems are designed to transmit data constantly, beginning about four hours before closest encounter. Because of Giotto's high speed, there is a real danger that a collision with a small particle of dust will knock the spacecraft's antenna out of alignment with Earth. This would mean a permanent loss of data. Unlike other probes, Giotto will not be able to store data to play back later. There probably won't be a "later" anyway, since the dust will probably destroy the craft sometime around closest approach.

Future Missions

The five Halley missions are just the beginning of our efforts to study comets in space. Though they will provide a flood of valuable new data, they are limited by their "flyby" paths. The next step will be a rendezvous with a comet.

A flyby is like an arrow passing a flying bird — the mission is over quickly, within a few hours. NASA is currently studying a mission in which a spacecraft will fly alongside a comet for several months in 1994. According to this plan, a Mariner Mark II craft will be sent to catch up with Comet Wild 2 before sunlight creates a bright coma and tails. Meeting the comet about Jupiter's distance from the Sun, it will travel to within about five miles of the comet. Pictures taken from this distance will reveal details on the nucleus as small as five inches across. Once the comet is activated by the Sun, the spacecraft will back off to a safe distance, where it will continue its observations.

Among other things, such a mission will provide measurements of the nucleus' mass. With this information, scientists will finally

The Canberra, Australia, station of NASA's Deep Space Network (DSN). The Deep Space Network, which includes stations in Spain and California, will track the Soviet Vegas. Precise information on the location of the Vegas is important for targeting the Giotto spacecraft.

NASA Photo

A Mariner Mark II could meet Comet Wild 2 in 1994 and fly alongside the comet for several months. The Mariner Mark II spacecraft, an ''economy model'' proposed by NASA, is designed to be used for many different types of missions.

NASA Art

be able to determine just how much ice and dust a comet contains. This will show whether comets really are ''dirty snowballs,'' or rocky objects merely covered with ice.

The next comet mission would probably be designed to collect samples of the nucleus, returning them to Earth for thorough study. It will probably be 20 years or more before a human sets foot on a comet (perhaps you will be one of the first!), but in the meantime, our robot space probes will advance comet science far beyond the wildest dreams of Edmond Halley.

Even when all the mysteries about comets are solved, the beauty of these celestial vagabonds will continue to excite their earthly admirers. They will remain a fascinating example of the complex ways nature creates beauty in the cosmos. And they will serve as a reminder of the tremendous satisfaction we can achieve when we accept the never-ending challenge of understanding the universe.

Chapter 6

The Return of Halley's Comet

You are about to take part in a tradition that stretches back at least 2,000 years. Your observations of Comet Halley put you in the company of ancient kings and famous astronomers.

We don't know how long Halley's Comet has been making its 76-year tour of the Solar System. So far, records of only 30 returns (counting this one) have been found.

The earliest mention of Comet Halley is by ancient Chinese astrologers, who noted the appearance of a "broom star" in 240 B.C. For a long time, Halley's return in 164 B.C. was a bit of a mystery. No record of the comet could be found, and astronomers wondered whether it was visible from Earth. In 1985, though, an astronomer and an archeologist reported that they'd discovered a reference to the comet in an ancient Babylonian tablet. With this finding, the record of Halley's last 30 returns is complete.

Calculations show that the best view of the comet came in 837 A.D. That year, the comet came within 5 million miles of our

One of the most famous appearances of the comet came in 1066, the year William the Conqueror invaded England. His victory over the English King Harold was commemorated in the Bayeux Tapestry, which includes a picture of Harold being warned of the comet's appearance — a bad omen (for Harold, anyway!).

From The Bayeux Tapestry. Copyright © 1966 Norman Denny & Josephine Filmer-Sankey. Used with permission of William Collins Sons & Company, Ltd., London.

The markings on this reproduction of an ancient Babylonian tablet contain detailed records of the return of Comet Halley in 164 B.C. Besides filling an important gap in the historical record of Halley, the descriptions on the tablet are useful in verifying the calculations of Halley's past orbits.

From *Late Babylonian Astronomical and Related Texts,* by Theophilus Pinches. Reprinted by permission of University Press of New England.

planet — the closest known approach — only about 40 days after perihelion.

From a scientific point of view, the most important return of Halley was the one predicted by Edmond Halley. The English astronomer calculated that the comet would reach perihelion in 1758. A German amateur astronomer made the first observation of the returning·comet on December 25, 1758. Perihelion came in March 1759.

Most popular ideas about Halley's Comet come from its spectacular appearance in 1910. That year the comet was large and bright, easily visible from any city. The tail stretched nearly two-thirds of the way across the sky! Besides attracting a lot of popular attention, the comet was studied closely by astronomers. In fact, most estimates of the comet's brightness during the 1985-86 return are based on observations made in 1910.

Now the comet is returning again. Using sensitive detectors and the 200-inch telescope on Mount Palomar, two astronomers "recovered" Halley on October 16, 1982, when the comet was 11 AU from the Sun — over three years before perihelion. The early recovery allowed astronomers to observe the comet before the nucleus became hidden by the coma, and to follow the development of the comet's coma and tails.

Besides observations by spacecraft, a worldwide network of professional and amateur observers will observe the comet. This return of Halley will be one of the most closely watched astronomical events in history.

The telescopes and space probes will produce fascinating photos of Comet Halley. But of course you're not going to sit around waiting for pictures when you can go out and see for yourself!

Now, the Bad News

All right. It's time to face the music: Despite all the excitement about the return of Halley's Comet, the fact is that this will be a poor appearance. One astronomer even said this return will offer "the worst viewing for the naked eye in the last 2,000 years"!

Halley's poor showing doesn't mean you should lock yourself in your room and play video games until it's gone! What it *does* mean is that you'll have to make a bit more of an effort to enjoy the comet than people did in, say, 1910. But before we see how to make the most of Halley's return, let's take a quick look at the reasons for the "Great Halley Fizzle."

You can't really blame the comet. Halley will probably shine as brightly, and sprout as fine a tail, as it did in 1910. If there's a culprit, it's our planet: It's in the right places at the wrong times.

Comet Halley and Earth move in opposite directions. This means that the comet will twice approach our planet, once before perihelion and once after. The first approach, occurring on November 11, 1985, brings the comet within about 68 million miles of Earth. Only about 1½ AU from the Sun, the comet will already be glowing, increasing in brightness as it nears the Sun. In fact, Halley will grow brighter in our sky *after* this close approach, because the comet is receiving more and more solar radiation as it approaches perihelion.

Around perihelion on February 9, 1986, the comet will be reflecting and emitting the maximum amount of light, but we won't be in a position to appreciate it. At that time, Halley will be about 144 million miles from us, and practically on the opposite side of the Sun — too far to appear very bright and too

ABOVE: These photos, taken in 1910, show the changing appearance of Halley's Comet over roughly six weeks.

Palomar Observatory Photographs

The Mawangdui Silk Book is an ancient Chinese catalogue of comet types used for astrology. The left comet foretold "internal war and a bumper crop"; the comet at right meant "small war and corn plentiful."

Redrawn from the *Mawangdui Silk Book*

close to the Sun to be seen from our point of view!

After perihelion, the comet and Earth again begin to approach one another. On April 11, Halley will be at its closest to Earth, about 39 million miles. The comet will *appear* brightest from Earth then, even though it actually emitted more light two months earlier, at perihelion. The comet will be easily visible to the naked eye, but only from dark sites; you'll probably need binoculars for a good look if you're in the city.

It's easier to appreciate these numbers by comparing this return with the return of 1910. That year the comet came within 15 million miles of Earth a little less than a month after perihelion.

Observers in the northern hemisphere will have the worst view in April, since Halley will be near or below the southern horizon when it is brightest. But it will quickly climb higher in the sky shortly after closest approach, and will be visible to the naked eye for nearly a month after that.

So conditions aren't great for anybody, and especially difficult for northerners. But don't give up: Everyone will still be able to get a good look at the comet — you'll be able to watch it for weeks! The trick is to make like a Scout and BE PREPARED!

Getting Ready for the Comet

Because Comet Halley is not likely to get very bright from our point of view, it's going to be a bit tougher to find than you might expect. To make the most of Halley's visit, you should start your preparations before the comet even becomes visible.

Scout around for dark observing sites. Really serious observers will want to get far away from city lights — a 30 minute drive

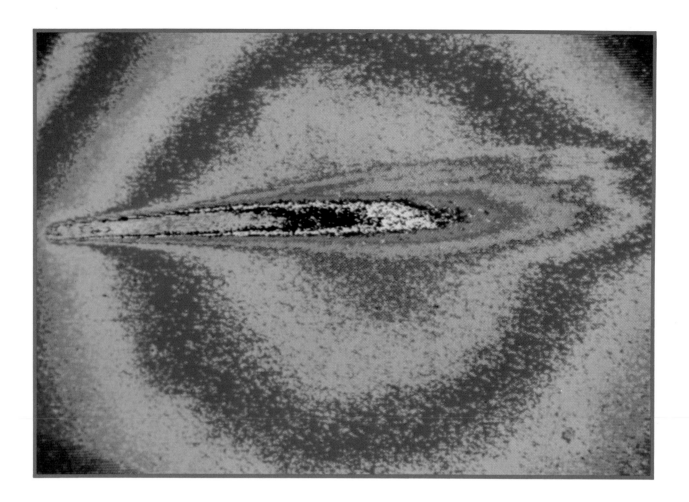

or more. Besides the lighting, pay attention to the horizon, since Halley will often appear low in the sky. Since there are basically two phases of the appearance — one before perihelion and one after — you may need two sites. The maps on the following pages show that the comet will appear in the western skies in December and January (before perihelion), and in the east and south after that. You may find that an observing site that's great for viewing Halley in January will be terrible in March and April.

As you look at the maps, see how many of the constellations you recognize. It's a good idea to spend some time getting to know the constellations that Halley passes through. If you know your constellations, it will be easier to spot Halley — it'll be the object that "doesn't belong there."

The 1910 return of Halley continues to provide information to astronomers. The color photos on these pages are 1910 Lowell Observatory photos that were image processed at Kitt Peak National Observatory. Such computerized processing often reveals detail hidden in the original image.

National Optical Astronomical Observatories and Lowell Observatory Photos

Equipment

You'll be seeing a lot of advertisements for "Comet Telescopes." In fact, a pair of 7 X 35 or 7 X 50 binoculars is all you need for a good look at the comet. Used in a dark site, binoculars should reveal the comet by around mid-November.

A telescope will be handy before December 1985 and after May 1986, when the comet will be small and faint. When the comet is at its biggest and brightest, a telescope's field of view will be too small to include the entire comet. However, a telescope will allow you to see the fainter portions of the tail that binoculars won't reveal. Use the lowest possible magnification (or "power"); the image will be brighter, and more of the comet will fit into the field of view.

The only other equipment you'll need are the maps in this book

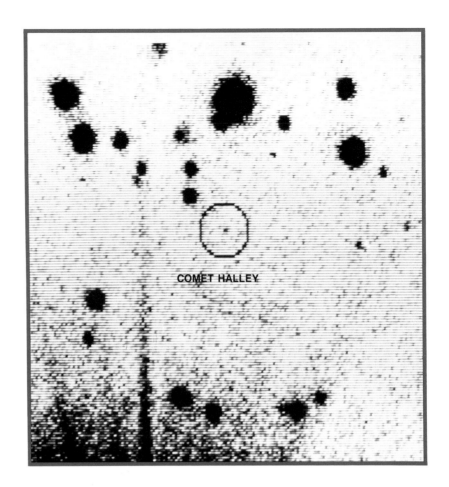

This is the first image of Comet Halley since it faded from view in 1911. Using a detector designed for the Space Telescope, astronomers David Jewett and G. E. Danielson captured the image at the 200-inch Hale Telescope on Mount Palomar on October 19, 1982. When the image was made, Halley (in circle) was 100 million times fainter than it will be in April 1986.

Courtesy Jet Propulsion Laboratory

COMET HALLEY

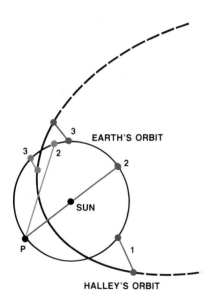

This diagram shows the positions of the Earth and Comet Halley in 1910 and 1986. The blue dots show the 1986 positions during first approach (1), perihelion (2), and second approach (3). The gray dots show the 1910 positions at perihelion and closest approach (2 and 3). "P" marks the comet's position at perihelion.

and a light to read them by. Any flashlight will do, but you should cover the lens with red cellophane or several layers of paper from a grocery bag. This will create a dim red light that will let you see the maps without ruining your night vision. (After about 30 minutes in the dark, your eyes' pupils are open widest, allowing you to see faint objects — like the comet. Any bright light will make your pupils shrink in an instant, and you'll have to wait another half hour for your eyes to adjust fully to the dark.)

What to Look For

Don't be satisfied with (or disappointed by!) just one look at the comet. It will go through many interesting changes during the weeks before and after perihelion. You can watch the tail and coma grow. Also, keep an eye out for changes in detail in the coma and tail. Comets can change appearance suddenly, so observe Halley as often as possible — you don't want to miss anything!

You'll also be able to watch Halley wander through the stars from night to night. Sketches of the comet will record the movement, as well as changes in the comet itself.

Comet Halley is a link to the past and the future: Every 76 years, this beautiful wanderer invites the people of the world to stop and together turn their minds from the worries of our planet to the universe beyond. As we gaze into space, we are reminded that we share a small place in space and time. And with hundreds of scientists worldwide joining together to study the comet, it's nice to know that Halley has finally become a symbol of international cooperation, rather than a sign of natural disasters and war.

The View From the Northern Hemisphere

In November 1985, amateur astronomers will be able to get their first look at Comet Halley in 75 years. You'll probably need at least a 60mm telescope to find the faint fuzzy smudge of light between the horns of Taurus, the Bull. By the time the comet lies below the bright cluster of stars known as the Pleiades, you should be able to spot it with binoculars from a dark site. After that, you can watch for the developing coma and growing tail. After the comet has passed beneath the Great Square of Pegasus in late December, it should be visible to the naked eye from very dark observing sites. Binoculars will still be your best bet, though.

Hold the chart overhead so that the direction on the chart matches the direction you're facing.

This map shows how the sky appears at:
- 1:30 a.m. on October 1
- 11:30 p.m. on November 1
- 9:30 p.m. on December 1
- 7:30 p.m. on January 1

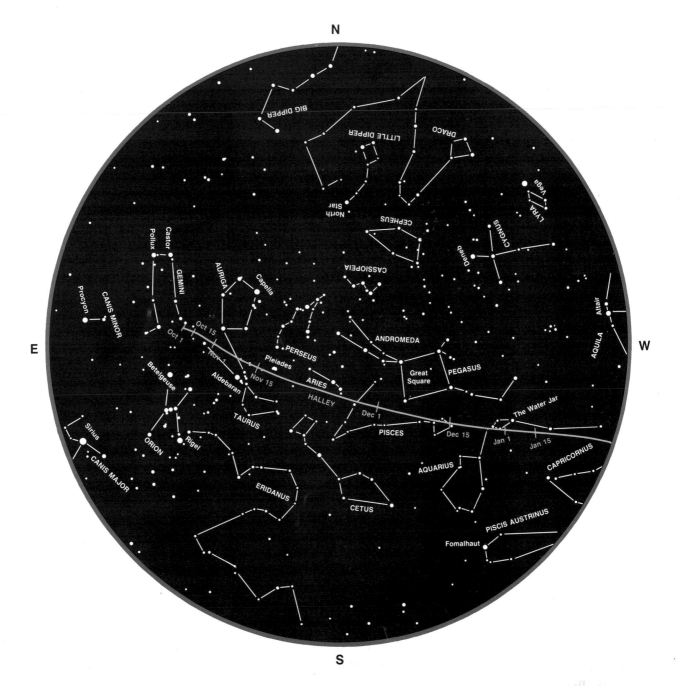

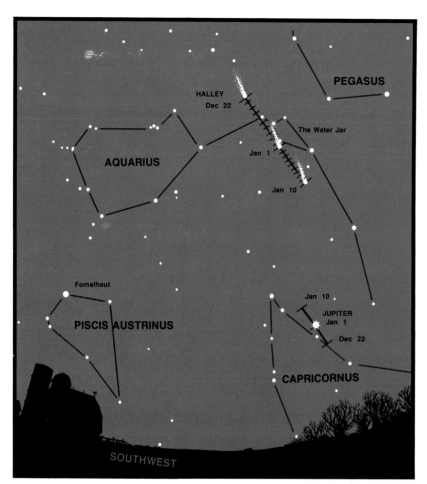

December 22, 1985, to January 10, 1986
1½ Hours After Sunset

The planet Jupiter is your guide for finding Halley. Look to the southwest for a bright yellowish "star" — that's Jupiter. You'll find the comet right above the planet, near a Y-shaped group of faint stars known as the "Water Jar." The comet might be tough to spot before the 28th, since the bright Moon will be nearby. Try to memorize the location of the Water Jar below the Great Square of Pegasus — it will help you find Halley later in the month.

Maps by Frank Reddy

January 10 to January 25, 1986
1½ Hours After Sunset

Halley is picking up speed as it nears the Sun. The comet is catching Jupiter, but the planet will be hard to spot by the time the sky is totally dark. If you can't find Jupiter, look to the right of the Moon, below the Water Jar. The light of the young Moon will make Halley tough to spot by the middle of January, so use binoculars if you can. By the end of the month, the comet will be too close to the Sun to be visible. The comet will reappear in the morning sky in mid-March.

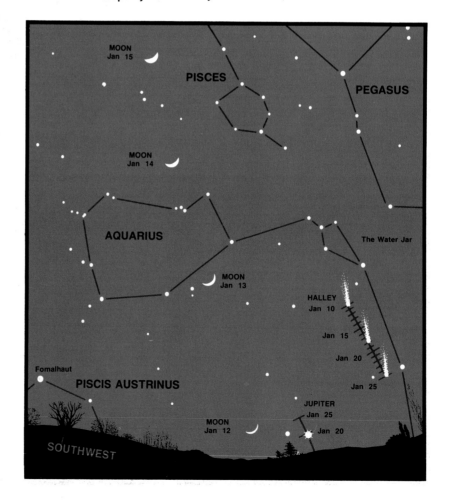

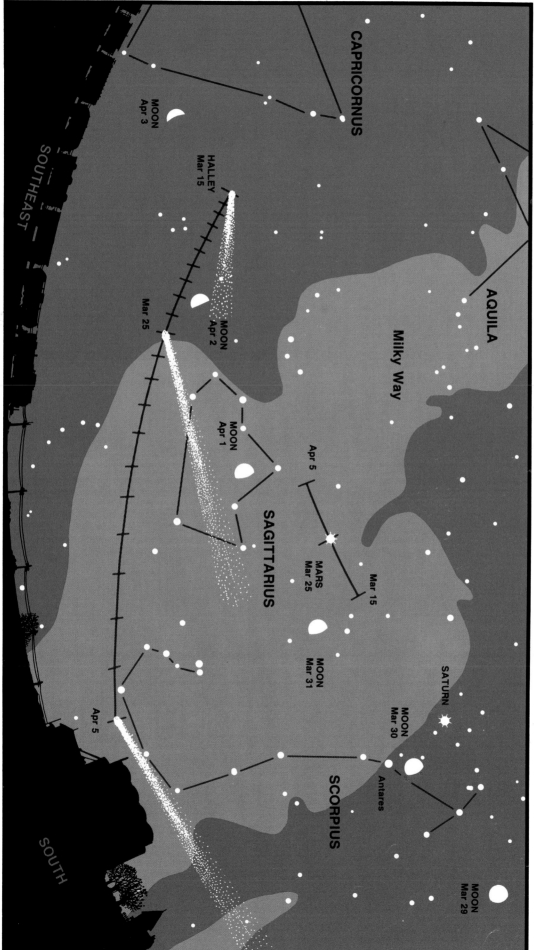

March 15 to April 6, 1986, About 2 Hours Before Sunrise

Comet Halley has now passed around the Sun, but it is also heading for the southern sky. Look for it low in the southeast, below and to the left of Mars and Saturn, the two "stars" near the horizon. Earth and the comet are traveling roughly toward each other, so the comet is moving swiftly through the sky. The comet is growing brighter rapidly and its tail is getting longer. Unfortunately, moonlight will wash out most of the comet's light as it passes below Sagittarius. Notice that the tail is *in front* of the comet as it travels away from the Sun.

CAPRICORNUS

MOON
Apr 3

SOUTHEAST

HALLEY
Mar 15

MOON
Apr 2

Mar 25

AQUILA

Milky Way

MOON
Apr 1

Apr 5

SAGITTARIUS

Mar 15

MARS
Mar 25

MOON
Mar 31

SATURN

MOON
Mar 30

Apr 5

SCORPIUS

Antares

SOUTH

MOON
Mar 29

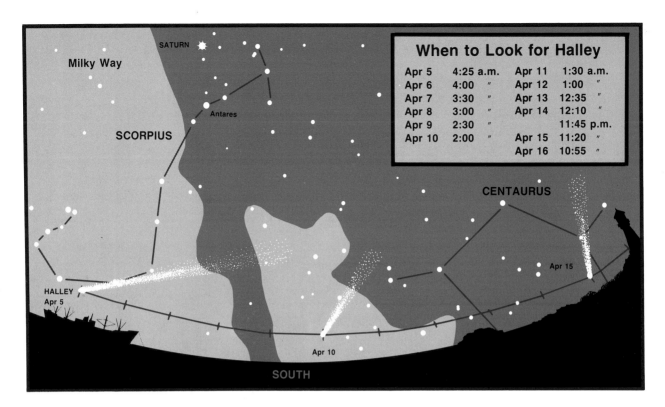

When to Look for Halley

Apr 5	4:25 a.m.	Apr 11	1:30 a.m.
Apr 6	4:00 "	Apr 12	1:00 "
Apr 7	3:30 "	Apr 13	12:35 "
Apr 8	3:00 "	Apr 14	12:10 "
Apr 9	2:30 "		11:45 p.m.
Apr 10	2:00 "	Apr 15	11:20 "
		Apr 16	10:55 "

April 5 to April 16, 1986

(See Table Above For Times)

Halley is now racing past the Earth, making its closest approach on the 11th. Though the comet is above the horizon for observers in the U.S., the thick atmosphere will probably block out all but the upper parts of the comet's tail. The table above tells when the comet lies due south — the best time to look. You'll find the comet below Saturn and Antares, the bright reddish star in Scorpius. Watch as the tail turns and shrinks beginning around the 10th. The Moon's light will interfere with viewing after the 16th.

April 17 to August 1 Evening Twilight

Earth and Halley are now speeding away from one another, causing the comet to fade rapidly. The Moon will interfere with observing until about the 25th, and again after May 13. As the comet's distance increases, it will appear to move more slowly through the sky. By mid-May, you'll need binoculars to spot the comet; a telescope will be necessary by July. With a 4-inch or larger telescope, you may be able to watch the comet until early August, when it heads into the daytime sky.

The View From the Southern Hemisphere

Unlike those in the Northern Hemisphere, southern observers probably won't get a good naked-eye view of Comet Halley before March 1986. On October 1, 1985, Halley rises in the northeast at about 1:00 a.m. As the comet heads west into the evening sky, the short nights of summer won't provide much opportunity to see the comet high above the horizon. By the time Halley reaches the limit of naked-eye vision, toward the end of December, southerners will need binoculars: The comet will be appearing in the twilight sky, where its own dim light will be blanketed by the fading light of the Sun. When the sky is dark enough for a good look, Halley will be very close to the horizon, and the comet's dim light will fade as it passes through the Earth's thick atmosphere. Though the pre-perihelion observing is poor, your view of Halley after perihelion will be worth the wait!

Hold the chart overhead so that the direction on the chart matches the direction you're facing.

This map shows how the sky appears at:

1:30 a.m. on October 1
11:30 p.m. on November 1
9:30 p.m. on December 1
7:30 p.m. on January 1

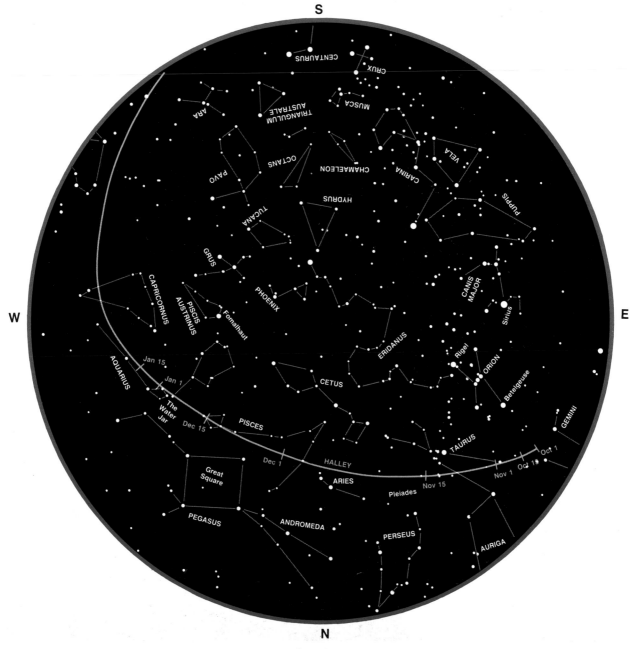

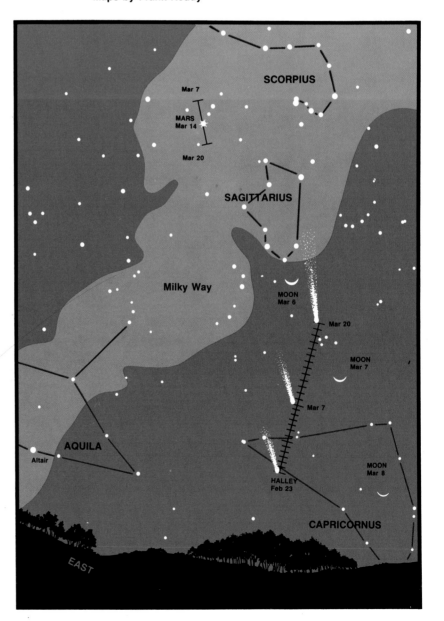

December 22, 1985, to January 10, 1986 2 Hours After Sunset

By the time the sky is completely dark, Halley will be low in the west. With the help of binoculars, you'll find it to the right of the bright "star" Jupiter. Moonlight will brighten the sky — and make the comet tough to spot — until around December 29. By mid-January, Halley will probably set before the sky is dark enough for you to spot it.

Maps by Frank Reddy

February 23, 4:45 a.m. March 1, 4:15 a.m. March 15, 3:15 a.m.

Halley has rounded the Sun and is much brighter than the last time you saw it. The comet will first appear to the right of the bright star Altair about an hour before sunrise. Moonlight and the sunlit glow of dawn will make the comet hard to spot before March 9. As the comet travels higher into the sky, you'll be able to watch it earlier and earlier in the morning. Watch Halley's tail lengthen as the comet moves up toward the reddish "star" Mars. The comet may grow a bit dimmer as it speeds away from the Sun.

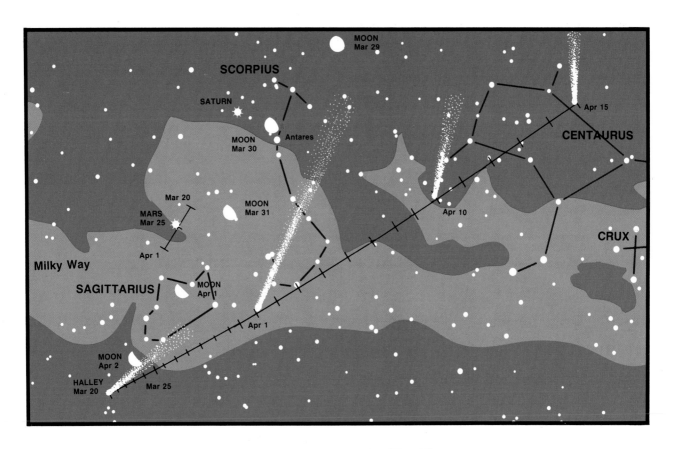

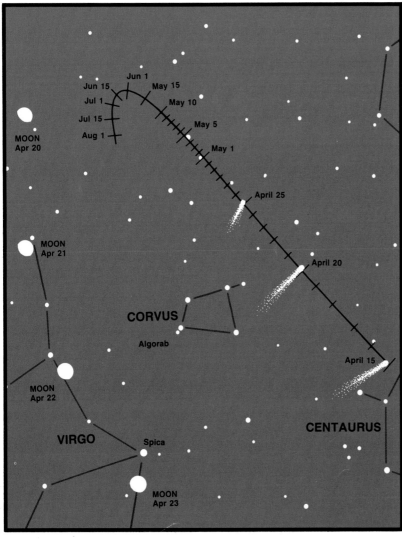

March 20 to April 16

The comet now begins to brighten as it nears Earth. In late March, Halley rises at midnight, and is overhead as dawn breaks. As the comet passes to the south of Mars, Saturn, and Antares, it becomes brightest, and its tail is longest. Unfortunately, the Moon's light will wash out Halley at its best. By April 10, the comet rises at sunset and is visible all night long. Notice how the tail turns and shrinks beginning around April 10.

April 17 to August 1

As the comet fades, it begins to move more slowly through the stars. In mid-April, the comet appears in the east about 2 hours after sunset. Observers in Australia and New Zealand will see an eclipse of the Moon on April 24, which will allow a last good look at the comet. You'll probably need a telescope to see Halley by July. By early August, Halley has passed into the daytime sky.

49

BUILD·A COMET!

By Mary Algozin

Glowing against the blackness of space, our comet whizzes toward the Sun! Make this model for a science fair project or for classroom display — you'll learn a lot about the structure of comets as you do!

You Will Need:

- Corrugated cardboard box, about 2 feet by 1 foot by 1 foot
- Black poster paint
- 1-inch-wide paint brush
- Optional: white poster paint and an old toothbrush
- Wooden dowel ¼ inch in diameter, about 30 inches long
- "Grain-of-wheat" lightbulb — a small 12-volt lightbulb, already wired, usually used in model railroad layouts (available at a hobby shop)
- Clear, hard plastic charm container from a 25-cent charm machine (or any similar container about 2 inches high)
- Icepick, skewer, or awl
- Black single-conductor hook-up wire (available at a toy or hobby shop)
- Single-pole, single-throw knife switch or any other simple on-off switch (look in a hardware store or an electronics supply store)
- Three 9-volt batteries
- Black electrical tape
- Cellophane tape
- Box of sterile cotton (available at a drugstore)
- Black construction paper
- Glue
- Black thread

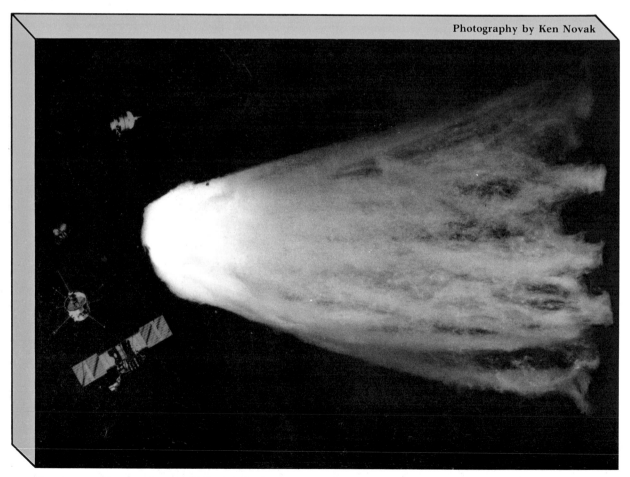

Photography by Ken Novak

Directions

1 Cut the flaps off the box. Paint it inside and out with black poster paint. Let it dry thoroughly. If you wish, you can paint stars all over the inside of the box. Here's how: Put a little white poster paint on a saucer. Dip the bristles of an old toothbrush into the paint. Hold the toothbrush about 4 inches from the box and run your thumb along the bristles so that the paint spatters onto the box in a random way. (Practice this technique on scrap paper or newspaper before you try it on your comet box!) Allow the stars to dry thoroughly before continuing.

2 Paint the dowel black and allow it to dry thoroughly. Cut the dowel about ¼ inch longer than the box. Trim it so that it fits snugly inside the box the long way — leave it long enough so that the box itself holds the dowel in place.

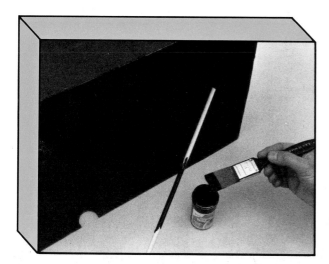

3 Heat the skewer or icepick and use it to make a hole in the top and bottom of the plastic container. The holes should be just big enough to allow the wooden dowel to go through. (You may need an adult's help for this step!)

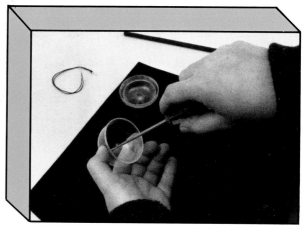

4 Cut two pieces of black hook-up wire about 36 inches long. Trim about ½ inch of insulation from the ends to expose the copper wire underneath.

5 The little lightbulb will represent the comet's glowing nucleus. There are two wires connected to the bulb. Take the end of one wire coming from the lightbulb, twist it together with the copper at one end of the hook-up wire, and wrap a 1-inch piece of electrical tape snugly around them. Do the same with the other piece of hook-up wire and bulb wire.

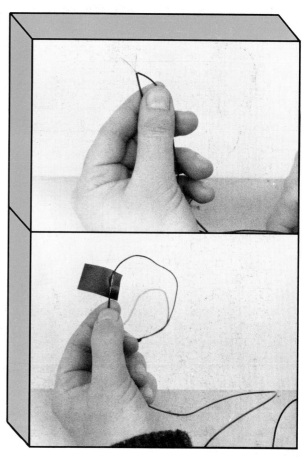

6 Tape the bulb to the dowel about ⅓ of the way down its length.

7 Thread the bottom of the plastic container down the short end of the dowel until it encloses the lightbulb. Thread the container's lid up the other end of the dowel. Close the container around the bulb *carefully*, so you don't damage the wire.

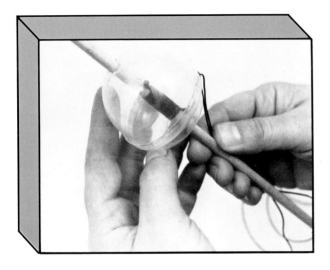

8 Stand the box on end. Slide the dowel to the center of the box. It should stay in place by itself. Wrap the wires coming from the lightbulb down and around the dowel and lead

them out the front of the box. Fasten the wire to the box with electrical tape.

9 Now you'll work on the cotton that will represent the comet's coma and tail. Unroll the cotton, cut a piece about 18 inches long, and peel off a thin layer.

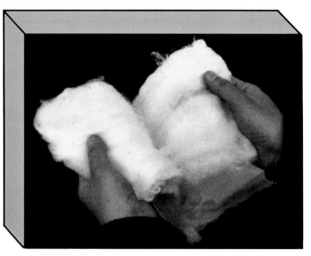

10 Carefully spread the cotton apart with your fingertips. You want to make it into a thinner sheet that has an uneven texture. If you happen to tear it, just take another piece and try again. (Fortunately, there's a lot of cotton in a box!)

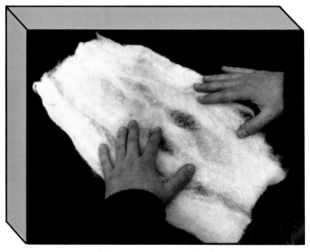

11 Drape the cotton around the front part of the plastic container and fasten it to the back of the container with a piece of electrical tape.

12 Tape down the comet's tail in about four places. This will help the comet keep its shape when you turn the box on its side. Carefully pull out little wisps of cotton from your comet's surface. Pull other scraps of cotton into long wispy shapes and put them on your comet — they'll stick by themselves.

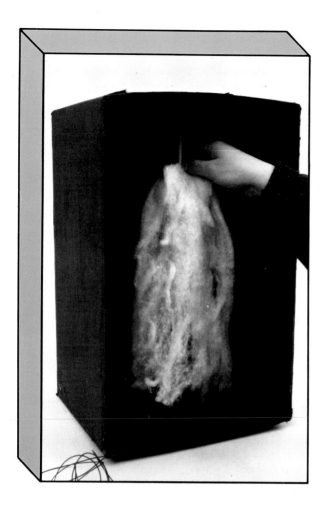

13 Now it's time to make your comet glow. Take one of the wires coming from the comet and cut it about 3 inches from the front of the box. Strip about ½ inch of insulation from both ends. Attach the ends to the two terminals of your switch. With most switches, you do this by tightening little screws against the bare wire. Put the switch in the "off" position.

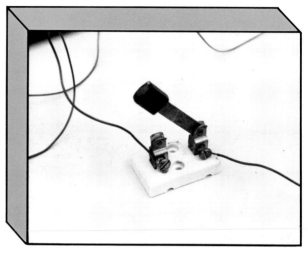

14 Take a close look at one of the batteries. You'll see that each battery has two terminals. One terminal is labeled positive (+), the other negative (−).

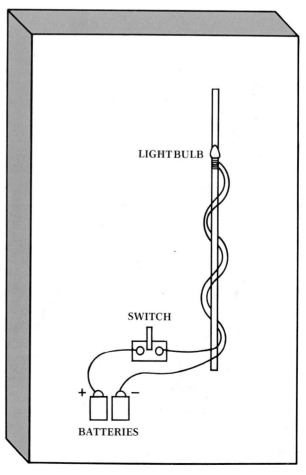

LIGHT BULB

SWITCH

+ −

BATTERIES

15 Take the two free ends of the wires coming from the comet. (One of these wires now has the switch attached.) Attach one wire to the *positive* terminal of one battery. Wrap it around the terminal and across the top of the terminal. Fasten the wire in place with a piece of electrical tape. Attach the other wire to the *negative* terminal of another battery.

16 Put the third 9-volt battery upside-down across the other two batteries so that its positive terminal snaps onto one battery's negative terminal and its negative terminal snaps onto the other battery's positive terminal.

17 We completed our comet model with pictures of the probes that will be investigating Halley's Comet. You can, too! Use the illustrations in Chapter 5 to draw small models of the comet probes. Cut out your probes and glue them to black construction paper (rubber cement works best). When the glue is dry, carefully cut them out. Cut four pieces of black thread about 10 inches long. Attach one piece of black thread to the back of each probe with cellophane tape. Attach the other end of the thread to the inside top of the box, adjusting the thread so the probes hang at different levels.

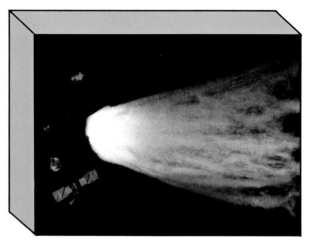

18 Flip the switch to the "on" position. There's your comet, coursing brightly through the heavens!

Another Source of Power

If you use three 9-volt batteries to light your comet, as we suggest in the instructions, you should not leave the comet turned on for long periods of time — the batteries will run down and the light will grow dimmer. The light will last longer if you use two 6-volt lantern batteries as your power source. They are more expensive than the 9-volt batteries, but worth the expense if your comet model will be getting a lot of use.

Here's how to use the lantern batteries: When you reach step 15, take the two free ends of the wires coming from the comet (one of these wires now has the switch attached). Attach one wire to the positive terminal of one battery. Wrap the copper end of the wire around the terminal spring and tape it in place. Attach the other wire to the negative terminal of the other battery. Cut a piece of hook-up wire about 12 inches long. Strip about ½ inch of insulation from both ends. Attach one end of this wire to the negative terminal of the first battery, and the other end to the positive terminal of the second battery. Then proceed with step 17.

Looking for Meteors

Most years don't bring a bright comet for stargazers to enjoy. And even a famous comet like Halley isn't always as spectacular as we would like. But comets can provide hours of fun long after they have disappeared from sight. The meteor showers created by trails of comet dust provide us with several special nights each year.

Observers have discovered over 20 annual meteor showers. Many are rather weak, with only a few dim meteors every hour. But there are several reliable showers — at least one per season — that deliver lots of bright meteors. The chart on the next page lists the best showers.

While the showers themselves are pretty reliable, observing conditions vary from year to year. Clouds or the Moon can spoil a shower (the moonlight will "wash out" all but the brightest meteors). And the peak of the shower — the time when Earth is passing through the thickest part of the stream — may occur during daylight hours. A good astronomical magazine (such as *Odyssey, Astronomy,* or *Sky and Telescope*) will help you decide whether a shower is worth watching in a given year.

You don't need any fancy equipment to enjoy meteors. In fact, all you need are your eyes and a little patience. Go outside on a clear, moonless night and look up. On an average night you'll see about eight visitors from space streak through the sky every hour. These are *sporadic* (spoh-RAD-ick) meteors. During a meteor shower, however, you can see as many as 60 an hour, sometimes more.

Because a meteor shower is a special event, experienced observers make some simple

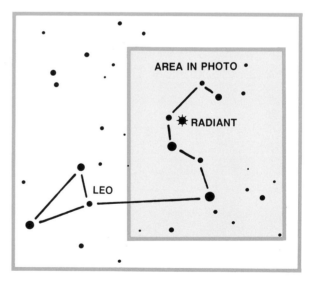

The Leonid meteor shower of 1966 put on a brief but spectacular display. This photo of the radiant in Leo's head (see diagram) caught 70 meteors in only 3½ minutes! The two white spots are "point meteors," meteors which were traveling right at the camera, and so showed no trails.

Photo by Dennis Milon

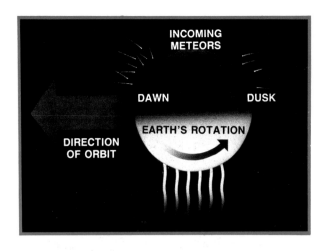

The diagram above shows why we see more meteors just before dawn: Earth is plowing right into the meteor stream, and the combined motions of Earth's spin and orbital speed increase the relative speed of the meteoroid. This makes it more likely that an incoming meteoroid will get hot enough to become a glowing meteor.

preparations. First of all, you have to dress more warmly than you think: Even mild summer air can seem chilly after you've been out for a while.

Spread a heavy blanket or sleeping bag on the ground (lying on your back will save a lot of neck strain!). A folding lounge chair is even better, since it will keep you off the cold, damp ground.

You can look for meteors any time after dark, but the phase of the Moon will help you decide when to look. When the Moon is new, you can look any time; the first quarter Moon will light up the sky until around midnight; a full Moon ruins the whole night; a last quarter Moon doesn't rise until midnight, so you can observe until then.

Meteor-watching is best just before dawn. (Of course, the Moon must be near new or first quarter phase.) That's when the atmosphere above you catches the most meteoroids,* because it is facing the direction of Earth's motion. (The same effect occurs on the highway: You see more dead bugs on a car's windshield than on the side or back windows.) If the phase of the Moon is right, you may decide to go to bed early and set your alarm for 3:30 a.m. (Check the weather forecast first to make sure it won't be cloudy!)

The meteors in showers appear to come from one spot in the sky, called the radiant. This is only an optical illusion: Like railroad tracks, the orbits of meteoroids are parallel; and like railroad tracks, they appear to meet in the distance.

Surprisingly, you won't see many meteors near the radiant. Meteors don't begin to glow until they have traveled some distance through the atmosphere, so look about 45 degrees from the radiant. (Forty-five degrees is half the distance from the point overhead to the horizon.)

It's fun to record your observations, and it's easy to do. You'll need a dim light that won't dazzle your dark-adapted eyes, so cover a flashlight with some red tissue or paper from a brown bag. Next, trace a star map that includes the constellation where the radiant is found — the shower's name usually comes from the constellation. (Try to use a map that shows the sky for the time you'll be observing.) You can then use a ruler and pencil to mark a meteor's track and number it (your dim light will help). Your map will clearly show most meteors coming from the radiant.

Until a bit of space junk enters Earth's atmosphere and becomes a bright meteor, *it is called a* meteoroid.

SHOWER	RADIANT	PEAK	METEORS PER HOUR (PEAK)	COMMENTS	PARENT COMET
Quadrantids	Above Bootes	Jan. 3	110	nice trails	?
April Lyrids	Lyra	Apr. 22	12	bright	1861 I
Eta Aquarids	Aquarius	May 3-5	20	best southern shower	Halley
Delta Aquarids	Aquarius	July 29	20		?
Perseids	Perseus	Aug. 12	60	many bright	Swift-Tuttle
Orionids	Orion	Oct. 21	20		Halley
Geminids	Gemini	Dec. 14	60	many fireballs	1983 TB**

**Discovered by the Infrared Astronomical Satellite (IRAS) in 1983. Probably a burnt-out comet.

Just as parallel railroad tracks appear to meet in the distance, meteoroids traveling in parallel orbits appear to come from a single point in the sky.

Meteor-watching is easiest in a reclining lawn chair.

Artwork by Victor Costanzo

On another sheet of paper, draw three columns and label them *number*, *time*, and *comments*. Examples of comments are "bright," "long trail," or "sporadic." (Any meteor that doesn't come from the radiant is a sporadic.)

Meteor showers often become more active when the parent comet is passing near Earth. Two comets, and possibly three, pass near Earth in 1985 and 1986, and the four showers associated with these comets may increase in intensity. The maps on the following pages will help you observe these showers.

The most obvious showers to watch are those connected with Comet Halley: the Orionids and the Eta Aquarids. In 1985, the Orionids peak on October 20, when the Moon is at first quarter — perfect for early morning observing. The Eta Aquarids of 1986 will arrive about three weeks after Halley's closest approach. With the Moon at its new phase, conditions will be perfect for observing this shower. Compare your counts

with the normal rates listed at left to see whether the comet's return has made any difference.

The Perseids, the best known and most reliable shower, may also increase in intensity. The parent comet, Swift-Tuttle, was only seen once, in 1862. The comet should complete an orbit every 120 years, but it didn't arrive in 1982 as expected. It's still overdue, and may arrive any time, bringing an increase in the shower's activity.

The Draconid shower, which is caused by the comet Giacobini-Zinner, peaks on October 8 — only 29 days after the comet's closest approach to Earth. This shower, which is weak when the comet is far from Earth, may be spectacular in 1985. However, since the last quarter Moon will be in the sky in the early morning (when the shower peaks in North America), the best times for viewing will be the evenings of October 7 and 8.

DRACONIDS AND PERSEIDS ▶

This chart shows the sky at 10:00 p.m. on October 7 and 8, 1985 (for Draconids), and 2:00 a.m. on August 12, 1986 (for Perseids).

ORIONIDS ◀

This chart shows the sky at 5:00 a.m. on October 21, 1985.

Hold the chart overhead so the direction on the chart matches the direction you're facing.

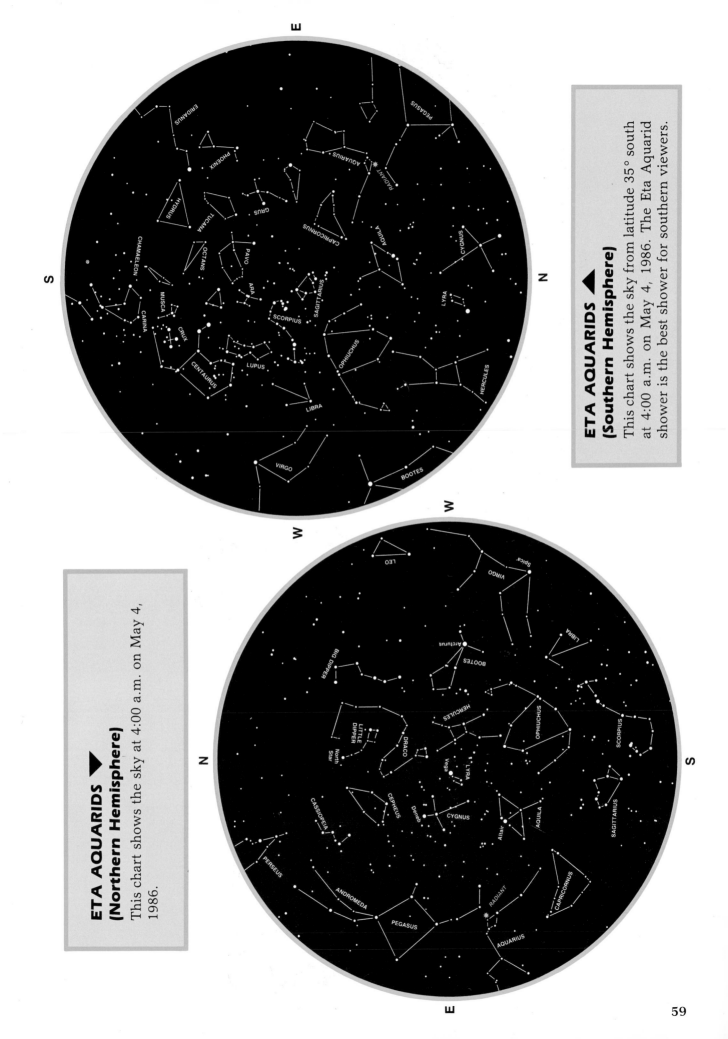

ETA AQUARIDS ▼
(Northern Hemisphere)
This chart shows the sky at 4:00 a.m. on May 4, 1986.

ETA AQUARIDS ▲
(Southern Hemisphere)
This chart shows the sky from latitude 35° south at 4:00 a.m. on May 4, 1986. The Eta Aquarid shower is the best shower for southern viewers.

The View From Space

By Tom Hunt and Frank Reddy

This three-dimensional model shows the positions of Earth and Halley's Comet during the comet's 1985-86 visit. It will help you picture just what's going on as the comet swings through our neighborhood!

YOU WILL NEED:
- Patterns on these pages
- Tracing paper
- Colored pencils or markers
- White tag board
- Rubber cement
- Scissors or razor knife

1 Trace the base, Earth's orbit, and Halley's orbit. (You may photocopy the parts instead.) Use colored pencils or markers to color in the bands at the edges of Earth's orbit and Halley's orbit. Be sure to note the colors in the key on Halley's orbit.

2 Glue the pieces to white tag board (rubber cement works best). When the glue is dry, carefully cut them out. Cut out the heavy black lines on each piece. (You may want to ask an adult for help in cutting the slots. A razor knife works best.)

3 Fold up all sides of the base. Insert the tabs into the matching slots and bend them back. Tape down the tabs on the inside of the base. (Do NOT fold or tape the triangles marked 1, 2, 3, 4.)

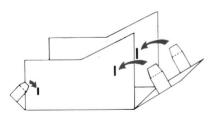

4 Insert Earth's orbit into the long slot in Halley's orbit. Make sure that Earth's orbit extends beyond Halley's orbit and that the half-circles at the center of each piece form a complete circle (the Sun).

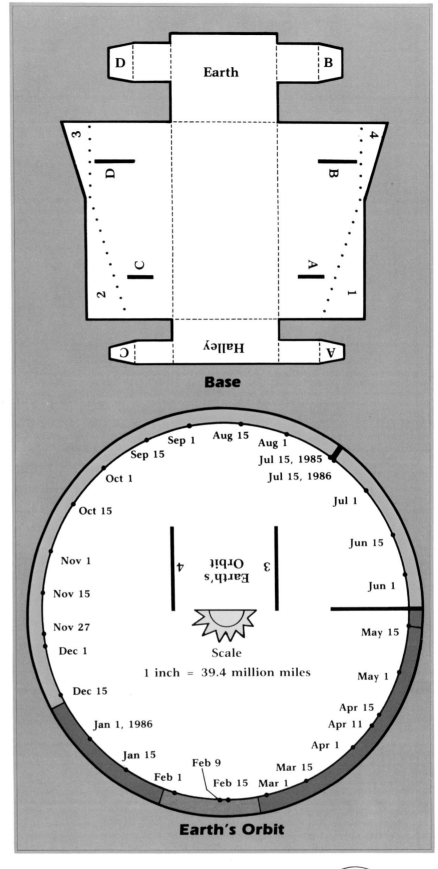

Base

Scale

1 inch = 39.4 million miles

Earth's Orbit

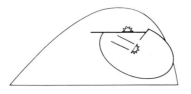
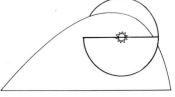

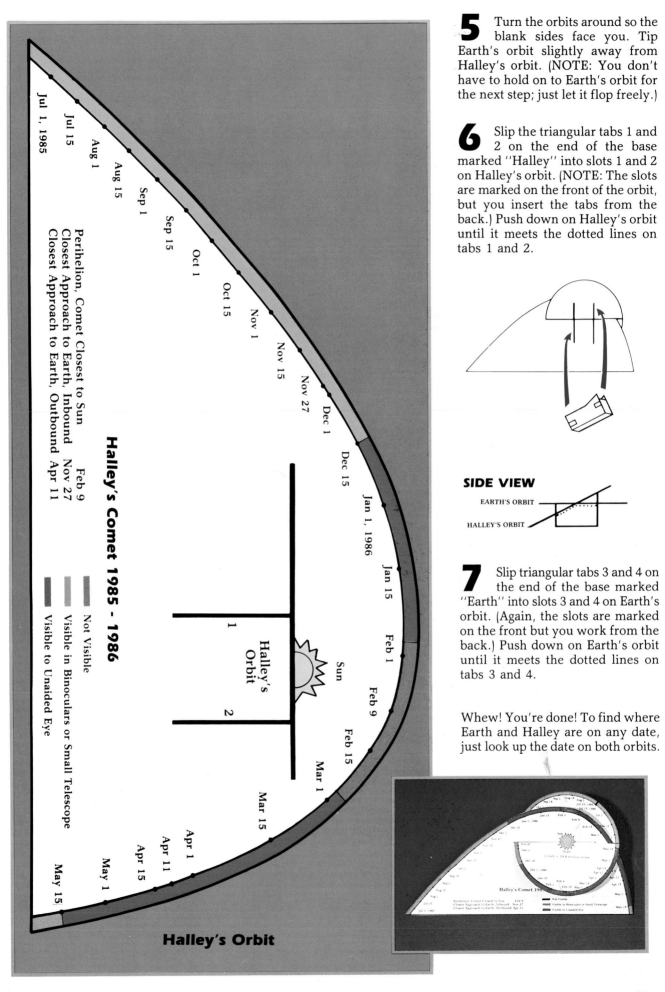

Halley's Comet 1985 - 1986

Perihelion, Comet Closest to Sun   Feb 9
Closest Approach to Earth, Inbound   Nov 27
Closest Approach to Earth, Outbound   Apr 11

Not Visible
Visible in Binoculars or Small Telescope
Visible to Unaided Eye

Jul 1, 1985
Jul 15
Aug 1
Aug 15
Sep 1
Sep 15
Oct 1
Oct 15
Nov 1
Nov 15
Nov 27
Dec 1
Dec 15
Jan 1, 1986
Jan 15
Feb 1
Feb 9
Feb 15
Mar 1
Mar 15
Apr 1
Apr 11
Apr 15
May 1
May 15

Halley's Orbit

Sun

Halley's
Orbit

1

2

5 Turn the orbits around so the blank sides face you. Tip Earth's orbit slightly away from Halley's orbit. (NOTE: You don't have to hold on to Earth's orbit for the next step; just let it flop freely.)

6 Slip the triangular tabs 1 and 2 on the end of the base marked "Halley" into slots 1 and 2 on Halley's orbit. (NOTE: The slots are marked on the front of the orbit, but you insert the tabs from the back.) Push down on Halley's orbit until it meets the dotted lines on tabs 1 and 2.

SIDE VIEW

EARTH'S ORBIT

HALLEY'S ORBIT

7 Slip triangular tabs 3 and 4 on the end of the base marked "Earth" into slots 3 and 4 on Earth's orbit. (Again, the slots are marked on the front but you work from the back.) Push down on Earth's orbit until it meets the dotted lines on tabs 3 and 4.

Whew! You're done! To find where Earth and Halley are on any date, just look up the date on both orbits.

Index

Glossary

Aphelion (ap-HEE-lee-un) — the point on a comet's or planet's orbit that is farthest from the Sun.

AU (Astronomical Unit) — the average distance between the Earth and Sun, about 93,000,000 miles (149,597,870 kilometers).

Coma (KOE-mah) — the huge cloud of dust and glowing gas surrounding the nucleus of a comet.

Direct orbit (also, **prograde orbit**) — counterclockwise orbital motion as seen from above the Sun. All the planets have direct orbits.

Dust tail — the stream of solid particles that trails behind a comet. Dust tails usually are curved, and form when the comet is about 3 to 5 AU from the Sun.

Gas tail — the stream of glowing gas that trails behind a comet. Gas tails are straighter than dust tails, and form when the comet is about 2 AU from the Sun.

Head — the coma and nucleus of a comet.

Hydrogen cloud — an invisible envelope of hydrogen gas surrounding a comet. A comet's hydrogen cloud can be many times larger than the coma.

Meteor — a piece of space debris that heats up and glows when it enters Earth's atmosphere. Before such a particle enters the atmosphere, it is called a **meteoroid**. Any part of a meteor that reaches the surface of the Earth is called a **meteorite**.

Nucleus (NEW-klee-uss); plural **nuclei** (NEW-klee-eye) — the solid core of a comet. Most astronomers believe that comet nuclei are made up of ices and dust — "dirty snowballs."

Nebula (NEB-you-lah); plural **nebulae** (NEB-you-lee) — a large cloud of gas and dust. The cloud from which the Solar System formed is known as the solar nebula.

Oort Cloud — the cloud of several million million comets that is thought to surround the Sun from about 20,000 to 200,000 AU. Jan Oort (yahn ort) proposed the cloud to explain comet orbits and the arrival of new comets.

Perihelion (pear-ih-HEE-lee-un) — the point on a comet's or planet's orbit that is closest to the Sun.

Period — the time taken by a planet, moon, or comet to complete one orbit.

Plane of the ecliptic — the imaginary flat disk on which Earth's orbit lies. The orbits of all the planets but Pluto lie very near the plane of the ecliptic.

Planetesimals (plan-eh-TESS-ih-mulls) — small clumps of dust and gas from which the planets formed during the earliest days of the Solar System.

Prograde orbit — see **direct orbit**

Retrograde orbit — clockwise orbital motion as seen from above the Sun; opposite the motion of the planets.

Solar wind — the flow of high energy particles from the Sun. The solar wind fills interplanetary space as far as 100 AU from the Sun.

Sublimate (SUB-lih-mate) — to change directly from an ice to a gas, without passing through a liquid state. The ices of comets sublimate to form the comas and gas tails. On Earth, the best example of sublimation can be seen in dry ice (frozen carbon dioxide).